CRANMER

and the

English Reformation

is one of the volumes
in the
TEACH YOURSELF HISTORY
LIBRARY

Edited by A. L. ROWSE

Teach Yourself History

VOLUMES READY OR IN PREPARATION

The Use of History, by A. L. Rowse
Pericles and Athens, by A. R. Burn
Alexander the Great and the Hellenistic Empire, by A. R. Burn
Constantine and the Conversion of Europe, by A. H. M. Jones
Charlemagne and Western Europe, by H. St. L. B. Moss
John Wycliffe and the Lollards, by K. B. McFarlane
Henry V and the Invasion of France, by E. F. Jacob
Joan of Arc and the Recovery of France, by Alice Buchan
Erasmus and the Renaissance, by Margaret Mann Phillips
Cranmer and the English Reformation, by F. E. Hutchinson
Raleigh and the British Empire, by D. B. Quinn
Laud and the English Church, by Norman Sykes
Cromwell and the Puritan Revolution, by Mary Coate
Gustavus Adolphus and the Thirty Years' War, by Raymond Carr
Richelieu and the French Monarchy, by C. V. Wedgwood
Milton and the English Mind, by F. E. Hutchinson
Peter the Great and the Russian Empire, by B. H. Sumner
Louis XIV and the Greatness of France, by Maurice Ashley
Wesley and the Methodist Movement, by Norman Sykes
Chatham and the British Empire, by Sir Charles Grant Robertson
Cook and the Opening of the Pacific, by James A. Williamson
Warren Hastings and British India, by Penderel Moon
Bolivar and the Independence of Spanish America, by J. B. Trend
Thomas Jefferson and American Democracy, by Max Beloff
Pushkin and Russian Literature, by Janko Lavrin
Livingstone and Central Africa, by Jack Simmons
Abraham Lincoln and the United States, by K. C. Wheare
Alexander I and the Rise of Russian Nationalism, by Michael Vyvyan
Gladstone and Modern Liberalism, by J. L. Hammond
Clemenceau and the Third Republic, by J. Hampden Jackson
Woodrow Wilson and American Liberalism, by E. M. Hugh-Jones
Lenin and the Russian Revolution, by Christopher Hill
Botha, Smuts and South Africa, by Basil Williams
Gandhi and Modern India, by Guy Wint

CRANMER
and the
English Reformation

by

F. E. HUTCHINSON, D.Litt., F.B.A.

(formerly Fellow of All Souls College, Oxford and Canon of Worcester)

ENGLISH UNIVERSITIES PRESS LTD.
AT SAINT PAUL'S HOUSE
IN THE CITY OF LONDON

First Printed . . 1951

All rights reserved

PRINTED AND BOUND IN ENGLAND
FOR THE ENGLISH UNIVERSITIES PRESS, LTD.,
BY HAZELL, WATSON AND VINEY LTD., AYLESBURY

A General Introduction to the Series

THIS series has been undertaken in the conviction that there can be no subject of study more important than history. Great as have been the conquests of natural science in our time —such that many think of ours as a scientific age *par excellence*—it is even more urgent and necessary that advances should be made in the social sciences, if we are to gain control of the forces of nature loosed upon us. The bed out of which all the social sciences spring is history; there they find, in greater or lesser degree, subject-matter and material, verification or contradiction.

There is no end to what we can learn from history, if only we would, for it is coterminous with life. Its special field is the life of man in society, and at every point we can learn vicariously from the experience of others before us in history.

To take one point only—the understanding of politics: how can we hope to understand the world of affairs around us if we do not know how it came to be what it is? How to understand Germany, or Soviet Russia, or the United States —or ourselves, without knowing something of their history?

GENERAL INTRODUCTION

There is no subject that is more useful, or indeed indispensable.

Some evidence of the growing awareness of this may be seen in the immense increase in the interest of the reading public in history, and the much larger place the subject has come to take in education in our time.

This series has been planned to meet the needs and demands of a very wide public and of education—they are indeed the same. I am convinced that the most congenial, as well as the most concrete and practical, approach to history is the biographical, through the lives of the great men whose actions have been so much part of history, and whose careers in turn have been so moulded and formed by events.

The key-idea of this series, and what distinguishes it from others that have appeared, is the intention by way of a biography of a great man to open up a significant historical theme; for example, Cromwell and the Puritan Revolution, or Lenin and the Russian Revolution.

My hope is, in the end, as the series fills out and completes itself, by a sufficient number of biographies to cover whole periods and subjects in that way. To give you the history of the United States, for example, or the British Empire or France, *via* a number of biographies of their leading historical figures.

GENERAL INTRODUCTION

That should be something new, as well as convenient and practical, in education.

I need hardly say that I am a strong believer in people with good academic standards writing once more for the general reading public, and of the public being given the best that the universities can provide. From this point of view this series is intended to bring the university into the homes of the people.

A. L. ROWSE.

ALL SOULS COLLEGE,
   OXFORD.

CONTENTS

I	THE ORIGINS OF THE REFORMATION	1
II	THE KING'S BUSINESS	19
III	THE REFORMATION PARLIAMENT	39
IV	THE DISSOLUTION OF THE MONASTERIES	64
V	THE ROYAL SUPREMACY	74
VI	THE ENGLISH BIBLE AND ENGLISH LITANY	89
VII	DURING SOMERSET'S PROTECTORATE	98
VIII	NORTHUMBERLAND'S RULE	115
IX	THE MARIAN REACTION	134
X	CRANMER'S TRIAL AND EXECUTION	149
XI	EPILOGUE	161

Chapter One

The Origins of the Reformation

THE immediate occasion of the Reformation in England was the insistent determination of Henry VIII to free himself at any cost from his marriage to Catherine of Aragon. The actual course of events which shaped the Reformation in England was greatly affected by this discreditable business and by the personalities concerned in it. The occasion is, therefore, important, but it should be distinguished from the more general and more deeply rooted causes which made some kind of reformation probable. Even so wilful and unscrupulous a Tudor monarch as Henry could not have effected his personal purpose if there had been a stiff resistance on the part of the English people to a rupture with Rome and if Henry had not been greatly helped by the manifestation in Europe of a general discontent with the medieval church system. The abuses of that system were admitted and deplored by good Catholics, who hoped for their removal by a vigorous reform movement within the Church.

The demand for a reform of the Church "in

Head and members" had been voiced for more than a century. The Papacy had lost not a little of its spiritual and moral authority. Its essentially supernational character had been weakened by the long residence of the Popes at Avignon (1309–76), which, though not in the realm of France, exposed them to undue French influence that could not be palatable to emperor or English king. And no sooner had "the Babylonish Captivity" ended than the Great Schism began and confused Christendom with rival Popes for the next fifty years (1378–1439). The Church Councils of Pisa (1409), Constance (1414–18) and Basle (1431–9) had disappointed the hopes of those who looked to them to effect administrative reform. The idea of subordinating the authority of the Pope to that of the Council failed to win general approval, and the Papacy emerged from the struggle with its autocracy re-established.

The splendour of the Renaissance Popes was dazzling, but their moral authority was lowered by the nepotism and profligacy of Alexander VI (Rodrigo Borgia, 1492–1503) and by the warlike propensities of Julius II (Giuliano della Rovere, 1503–13). The temporal power tended to divert the interest of a Julius II from the spiritual concerns of the Church to the political ambitions of an Italian prince. Leo X (Giovanni dei Medici, 1513–21), a patron of the arts and a lover of

THE ORIGINS OF THE REFORMATION

pleasure, and Clement VII (Giulio dei Medici, 1523–34), weak and vacillating, failed to initiate that reform from within the Church that might have saved it from the widespread break-up of Christian unity. It was already dangerously late when Paul III (Alexander Farnese), soon after his election in 1534, appointed a commission to report on the reform of the Church. The cardinals serving on the commission were mostly Italians with some width of view, like Contarini, and included with them was Reginald Pole, recently created a cardinal at the age of thirty-six. They produced a report which very frankly criticized the abuses and made drastic suggestions for reform. It is also noticeable that Contarini and Pole did not despair of an accommodation with the reformers across the Alps, even on such doctrinal matters as justification by faith. There followed in 1541 a conference between Catholics and reformers at Ratisbon, which failed perhaps for political as much as for theological reasons. Cardinal Caraffa, who had served on the commission, drew away and, as Paul IV, put the Consultum or report of the commission of 1538 on the Index. The conservatives had got the upper hand and reconciliation was no longer feasible. The Council of Trent, which met intermittently from 1545 (the year of Luther's death) to 1563, came too late to save the cause of Christian unity. It effected considerable reforms in discipline and administration, but its doctrinal definitions emphasized the irreparable cleavage beyond hope of conciliation. The Counter-Reformation strengthened the Church and purified it of many practical abuses; to this extent the Roman Church gained by the Reformation, and it aided the recovery of large parts of Europe to Catholic obedience.

The Renaissance also effected the transition from medieval to modern thought. In Italy, its original home, its leaders showed little interest in church reform. When the Popes were patrons of learning and the arts, the way was made easy for an accommodation with the Church by a none too serious conformity. A scholar might show up the falsity of the so-called Donation of Constantine, on which the extremer papal claims were commonly based, and yet be given and accept office in the papal court. But when the movement crossed the Alps, the scholars of the New Learning recognized its bearing on traditional beliefs and customs. Many of the Italians might be sceptical, but the more serious-minded Northerners betook themselves to the study of the Bible and the Fathers. Colet lectured on the epistles of St. Paul instead of the Schoolmen. Erasmus produced the Greek Testament with a new Latin translation, which corrected the Vulgate, the official Bible of the

THE ORIGINS OF THE REFORMATION

Church. When the New Testament was printed in vernacular translations, the contrast of its teaching with that of the contemporary Church was inescapable. Besides this important contribution to theological learning, Erasmus attracted popular attention all across Europe by his satirical writings. *The Praise of Folly*, written while he was Thomas More's guest at Bucklersbury, and his *Colloquies* (1516), the most popular book of the century, mercilessly ridiculed the intrigues and corrupt bargaining at papal elections, the venality of the papal court and "all their marketing of religion," the hawking of indulgences and relics, and the exploiting of popular superstitions by priests and friars. Erasmus even jested at the pretended knowledge of "our mincing schoolmen" about their explanations of the doctrine of transubstantiation. He might reasonably hope that the popular doctrinal excesses, which often outran official standards, might be corrected by the Church itself with the help of the New Learning and with the grateful approval of its loyal sons. It would be a mistake to infer that the New Learning would carry its adherents to the side of the Reformation. In fact, Erasmus drew back when he realized whither Luther was going, and, like More and many other humanists, valued the preservation of the Catholic unity more than immediate reforms.

CRANMER—THE ENGLISH REFORMATION

In England it was practical grievances against the Church, rather than doctrinal considerations, which produced anti-clerical feeling. The growth of national consciousness caused Englishmen to resent the payment of money to Rome and to regard papal collectors as foreigners. It was not King Henry only who considered royal authority impaired by the carrying of appeals to the papal court, with the consequent delays and uncertainty and the great expense. When the Pope "provided" non-resident foreigners to cathedral dignities and rich benefices, often at the expense of the rights of the native patrons, it stirred national resentment. With the growth of national expenditure and the unexpanding revenue of the Crown, covetous eyes were turned on the wealth of the Church, especially of the bishops and the monasteries. There were recent precedents for confiscation, or at any rate for the diversion of Church property from one purpose to another; Wolsey had obtained papal sanction for suppressing some twenty-two small monastic houses in order to endow his new colleges at Oxford and Ipswich. Thomas Cromwell, employed by Wolsey in this business, could hardly fail to suggest later to the King what possibilities there were of increasing the national revenue from such sources. The laity, too, might hope to gain lands and other property from such spoliation.

THE ORIGINS OF THE REFORMATION

There was also the very general feeling that the clerical order was not fulfilling its function adequately. Wolsey's own example was scandalous; to the archbishopric of York he added the see of Bath and Wells, which he exchanged for the much richer see of Durham, and in his last three years he held Winchester as well, besides having a great abbey and some preferments in France. Some of the diocesan bishops were seldom resident in their sees, being fully employed in the King's service as administrators of great offices of state or on foreign embassies. Many of the parish priests were pluralists and non-resident, while those who served their cures for them were negligent in preaching and some of them barely literate.

Anti-clerical feeling was specially stirred against the Church courts. Convocation had the right to pass canons (ecclesiastical laws) and attach penalties without the assent of King or Parliament, although the laity were affected. Probate of wills belonged to the courts spiritual, and there were many complaints of vexatious delays and excessive fees. It may, then, be understood what indignation was excited by the case of Richard Hunne, a merchant-tailor of London, in 1514. Soon after being confined to the Lollards Tower at St. Paul's on a charge of heresy, he was found hanging from a beam. At the coroner's inquest the jury accused the bishop's chancellor, his summoner and a bell-ringer of Hunne's murder, and they were committed to stand their trial. The bishop, Richard Fitz-James, at once appealed to Wolsey, asking him to get the King to have the matter inquired into by impartial persons, because he was sure that if his chancellor "be tried by any twelve men in London, they be so maliciously set in favour of heretical depravity that they will cast and condemn my clerk, though he were as innocent as Abel." The King ordered an enquiry, at which the plea of the accused that they were not guilty was accepted. Sir Thomas More, who was present at the enquiry unofficially, maintained many years after that Hunne was a manifest heretic and that he committed suicide. More is more likely to be right than the jury, but the main importance of the incident is that it shows the bishop's assessment of the feeling of the average London citizen.

There were not wanting voices from the clergy for the reform of discipline and moral standards. On 6th February, 1512, more than five years before Luther protested against the sale of indulgences, John Colet, dean of St. Paul's, preached at the opening of Convocation on the appointment of Archbishop Warham. In the previous year, twelve Lollards had been convented before Bishop Fitz-James; a rather larger number than in any previous year of his episcopacy. Ten of them had recanted, but two, who were relapsed heretics, had been burnt. Convocation was expected to deal expressly with the extirpation of heresy, but the preacher made only a passing reference to that subject. Instead he quoted St. Bernard as saying that the naughty life of the clergy does more harm to the Church than the words of heretics. He exhorted the reverend fathers "to the endeavour of reformation of the Church's estate, because that nothing hath so disfigured the face of the Church as hath the fashion of secular and worldly living in clerks and priests." He reproved the greed of the clergy for preferment, "that heaping of benefices upon benefices," the corruption and heavy exactions of the courts spiritual, the secular occupations of bishops and priests, and the admission of unfit and unlearned persons to holy orders. He asked indulgence for his outspokenness, representing himself as one "speaking of very zeal, a man sorrowing the decay of the Church." Seven years later Colet died, after having founded St. Paul's School. In his will, unlike his father or indeed Henry VIII, he left nothing for commemorative Masses. He desired that the Church should itself undertake the necessary task of reform. There is no reason to suppose that, had he lived to see the Reformation, he would have deserted the

Church any more than his friends, More and Erasmus.

All serious-minded Catholics recognized the current abuses and the need of reforming them. If the leaders of the Church had set their house in order before it was too late, they might have averted the avalanche which swept away both good and bad elements. Few will dispute that if a reformation could have been effected without sundering Christian unity, it would have been a better solution, although it remains arguable whether such a reform from within was possible. So far as it was a question of reforming practical abuses, vigorous Church action might have met the case, but it would prove infinitely harder if a reform of doctrine was urged. Crude popular distortions of official theology might indeed have been corrected and evidently superstitious usages discouraged, but reformers might demand more concession than the Church could make. It is natural to Englishmen to deal first with practical issues and to be slow in realizing their doctrinal significance. The actual evils of the sale of indulgences, for instance, were quickly perceived. Two years before Luther's protest, a young student at Cambridge denounced Leo X's proclamation on Indulgences which had been posted on the doors of the Schools by order of the Chancellor, Bishop Fisher. He was excommunicated by Fisher and fled overseas. More critical minds would be led to examine the theory of the treasury of merits, from which the Church held that indulgences were available. The devotion of so much time and money to the provision of Masses for the dead would inevitably provoke enquiry into the reasons for the belief in Purgatory and for the sacrificial character of the Mass. In fact, the nature of the Eucharist would become the most burning question of all, the dividing line between conservatives and reformers, as well as between the German and Swiss reformers. But in England, characteristically, the interest in doctrinal reform was for long confined to the few. One might expect the Lutheran doctrines to find a welcome among the surviving Lollards, but they did not reckon in their ranks any outstanding scholars in the universities or men in high place. From time to time obscure Lollards were arraigned before the bishops. A few were burnt in the reigns of Henry VII and Henry VIII, but most of them recanted and were condemned only to carry a faggot as a symbol of the punishment due to them under the heresy laws of Henry IV and Henry V. The Lollards were not numerous or influential enough to launch a reformation movement in England or even to lend any very valuable help to a movement introduced from abroad.

Luther's treatises began to be smuggled into England soon after their publication. The commercial intercourse between northern Germany and the east coast was constant, and traders as a class were early attracted to the Reformation. It is noticeable that even in the counties of Devon and Cornwall the seaports became centres of reforming activity. It was of greater importance that the universities were soon infected with the German teaching. As early as March, 1521, Archbishop Warham, Chancellor of Oxford, called Wolsey's attention to the danger. "I am informed," he writes, "that divers of the University be infected with the heresies of Luther and others of that sort, having a great number of books of the said perverse doctrine." By Wolsey's orders a pile of Lutheran books was burnt on Market Hill at Cambridge, and a similar burning took place in St. Paul's Churchyard in Wolsey's presence, while Fisher preached against "the pernicious doctrine of Martin Luther." At the same time the King was engaged in writing a Latin treatise controverting a work of Luther's in which the Pope's authority was repudiated and four of the seven sacraments were declared to be of only human origin. Henry's work, *Assertio Septem Sacramentorum*, was dedicated to Leo X, and a copy, bound in cloth of gold, was presented to the Pope by the English ambassador in Rome.

THE ORIGINS OF THE REFORMATION

On 11th October, 1521, a bull was promulgated conferring on Henry the title of *Fidei Defensor*. The title was presumably personal to Henry only, but, strangely enough, it has been assumed by every subsequent English sovereign.

But though Lutheran books were called in and burnt, and though the King had told Leo that "ever since he knew Luther's heresy in Germany, he had made it his study how to extirpate it," the books continued to find readers in the universities, especially at Cambridge. A few years later a group of like-minded friends were in the habit of meeting to discuss the new doctrines at the White Horse, which was significantly nicknamed "Germany." Robert Barnes, doctor of divinity, prior of the Austin Friars, was of the number, as was also another friar of that house, Miles Coverdale. "Little Bilney," a gentle soul, who had, like Luther, found comfort in the doctrine of justification by faith, though in other respects he appears to have been orthodox, frequented the White Horse. When Hugh Latimer delivered as his thesis for the degree of bachelor of divinity in 1524, a denunciation of Melancthon, Bilney sought him out and won him to his opinions. There were others in this group who afterwards, like Bilney, Barnes and Latimer, came to the stake. When in 1526 Wolsey sought to recruit promising young Cambridge scholars for his new foundation of Cardinal College at Oxford, it is remarkable that six of the eight who went to Oxford adopted reforming opinions. Indeed, the English Reformation ought almost to be called the Cambridge Movement.

There is no evidence of this group being joined by another Cambridge divine who was to play the most important part in the English Reformation. Thomas Cranmer was born in 1489 of gentle birth at Aslacton, a Nottinghamshire village. The brutal severity of his schoolmaster may be held partly answerable for a certain timidity that marked him throughout life, though he was from boyhood an intrepid horseman. At Cambridge he was in due course elected a Fellow of Jesus College, but forfeited his fellowship by marrying, while still a layman, a kinswoman of the landlady of the Dolphin, a respectable tavern near Jesus College. He then became a lecturer at Buckingham College, soon to be refounded as Magdalene. When his wife died about a year after in childbirth, his former college restored him to his fellowship. He gave himself wholeheartedly and contentedly to the study of divinity, took priest's orders and the degree of doctor of divinity, was appointed divinity lecturer of his college and examined in theology for the university; it is said that he exacted from the candidates for degrees a thorough knowledge of the Bible. He was of the scholarly

THE ORIGINS OF THE REFORMATION

type that comes slowly to conclusions and is at pains to know the best that is written on both sides of a controversial question. Even after his entry into public life, he continued the habits of a scholar and befriended scholars, whether English or continental. A scholar's life at Cambridge would have well contented him; it was not ambition that drew him into public affairs and to the precarious position of primate.

The cause of the Reformation in England was less advanced by Lutheran treatises than by the acquaintance of scholars with Erasmus' Greek Testament and his new Latin translation and, among the laity, by the translations of the Bible in the vernacular. Erasmus had said in the preface to his *Novum Testamentum*:

> The mysteries of kings it may be safer to conceal, but Christ wished his mysteries to be published as openly as possible. I wish that even the weakest woman should read the Gospel and the epistles of Paul... I long that the husbandman should sing portions of them to himself as he follows the plough, that the weaver should hum them to the tune of his shuttle, that the traveller should beguile with their stories the tedium of his journey.

It was perhaps the growth of Greek studies at Cambridge, after Erasmus had been Lady Margaret professor of divinity there for three years, that took William Tyndale to Cambridge after taking his master's degree at Oxford. Receiving priest's orders he served a Gloucestershire knight as chaplain. He expressed too frankly his amazement at the ignorance of the local clergy, and when one of them resented his language, he hotly replied: "If God spare me my life, ere many years I will cause a boy that driveth the plough shall know more of Scripture than thou doest." He repaired to London in the hope that Cuthbert Tunstall, the scholarly Bishop of London, would maintain him in his household while he translated the New Testament. The bishop was not unnaturally shy of adopting this unknown and vehement young man. Despairing of getting the help he needed in England, Tyndale went to Hamburg with the help of a London merchant, Humphrey Monmouth, who had heard him preach. With much difficulty he procured the printing of his New Testament, without his name being attached, and copies were smuggled into England and distributed by voluntary agents in Oxford and elsewhere. The bishops at once took alarm and required all who possessed copies to deliver them up under pain of excommunication, and the books were burnt at Paul's Cross. In the literary controversy which broke out three years later between More and Tyndale, the former maintained that a Bible in the vernacular was not against Catholic principle, but it should be "well

THE ORIGINS OF THE REFORMATION

and truly translated by some good and Catholic and well learned men," and it should be for the diocesan bishops to license those readers only who were fit. It is, however, the fact that in the fifty years during which printing had been exercised in England, no translation of the Bible had yet appeared, although the early printers produced translations of many other books of piety. Unfortunately, Tyndale's translations were accompanied by prologues to the different books incorporating much of Luther's own ideas. Still more unfortunately, some editions of Tyndale's had marginal notes that could not fail to be regarded as controversial; for instance, against the text "How shall I curse whom God curseth not?" is the note "The Pope can tell you how," and against "Meddle with your own business" is the note "A good lesson for monks and idle friars." It was not to be expected that the authorities of the Church would allow the circulation of Bibles with such notes and Lutheran prologues. Tyndale continued to print revised editions of his New Testament and some parts of the Old Testament. He was at last betrayed into the hands of Imperial officers who took him in May, 1535, to the State prison of the Low Countries in the castle of Vilvorde, near Brussels. There he lay for sixteen months before being brought to trial. An autograph letter of his to the Governor of the castle has survived:

> I entreat your lordship... to send me from my goods a warmer cap, for I suffer extremely from cold in the head... a warmer coat also... But above all I beseech your clemency to be urgent with the Procureur that he may kindly permit me to have my Hebrew Bible, Grammar and Dictionary, that I may spend my time with that study.

He was condemned for heresy and strangled at the stake before his dead body was committed to the flames on 6th October, 1536. His last words are reputed to have been, "Lord, open the King of England's eyes." Within a few years of his death the Great Bible, containing his version of the Pentateuch and the New Testament, was set up in every parish church.

Chapter Two

The King's Business

UNTIL the King and Parliament were committed to a policy that led to the repudiation of papal authority, the reform movement in England was confined to limited circles and might still have been crushed out by the ruthless use of force. The Reformation might, indeed, have later found powerful advocates in Church and State to ensure its success, but this could not be safely predicted, nor would it have taken the course it did but for Henry VIII's personal concern. Nothing seemed less likely than that the champion of orthodoxy, the Defender of the Faith, should himself for his own ends bring about the rupture with the Holy See.

At his accession in 1509, two months before he reached the age of eighteen, and for the first twenty years of his reign, Henry's orthodoxy was unimpeachable, and he stood in the graces of his subjects, both high and low. Six feet tall, athletic, handsome before he became corpulent, an intellectual, something of a scholar and the friend of scholars, he seemed to such men as Warham and

Erasmus a very paragon among princes. Nothing could explain his quarrel with Rome except the masterful strain in his character that would drive him to use any means whatever to obtain an object upon which he had set his heart. Cardinal Wolsey on his deathbed warned Sir William Kingston, in whose charge he was, of the obstinate self-will of the master he had served all too faithfully :

> He is a prince of royall courage, and hath a princely harte; and rather than he will miss or want any parte of his will or pleasure, he will endanger the losse of the one halfe of his realme. For I assure you, I have often kneeled before him, the space sometimes of three houres, to persuade him from his will and appetite: but I could never dissuade him therefrom. Therefore Mr. Kingstone, I warne you, if it chaunce you hereafter to be of his privy counsell, as for your wisdome ye are very mete, be well assured and advised, what ye put in his head, for ye shall never put it out againe.

All who had to deal with Henry soon knew his headstrong character, and few ever dared to cross him. Almost every official in Church and State who was drawn into Henry's matrimonial affairs —"the king's business," as it was discreetly called —suffered in character by their compliancy : Wolsey, Cromwell, Cranmer, Gardiner. In this ungenerous matter of Henry's desertion of a wife who had faithfully served him for nearly twenty years and borne him several children, though only one survived, it is fair to the King to state that his scruples about the marriage long preceded his infatuation for Anne Boleyn. Scruples had been entertained from the first project of the marriage. Henry's elder brother Arthur, Prince of Wales, died at Ludlow Castle at the age of fifteen years and a half, less than five months after his marriage to Catherine, daughter of Ferdinand and Isabella, who by their marriage had united the crowns of Castile and Aragon. Henry VII, desirous of continuing the Spanish alliance and, with his usual thrift, anxious to secure the dowry which had not yet been fully paid, was minded to contract the surviving son Henry to his brother's widow. Archbishop Warham was uneasy about it. Pope Julius II confessed to some doubt as to whether he was competent to dispense with the scriptural injunction "Whoso marrieth his brother's wife, he doth an unlawful thing (*rem facit illicitam*), he hath uncovered his brother's shame; they shall be childless." However, he gave the dispensation on 26th December, 1503. The future King was in his thirteenth year, and on the eve of his fourteenth birthday he protested that he would not ratify a contract made in his minority; probably he was prompted by his father, as Catherine's dowry was not yet secured. On 11th June, 1509, seven weeks after his coming to the throne, Henry VIII married Catherine, and for many years to come nothing more was heard of any scruple. But when, by 1514, all four of Catherine's children had been stillborn or had died in infancy, his superstitious feeling made him wonder if, after all, his marriage was unblessed by heaven and had earned the penalty—"they shall be childless."

The King, and indeed many of his statesmen, were by this time anxious about the succession. No one could contemplate without dismay a possible renewal of such civil war as had devastated England in the later half of the preceding century. And even when at last, in 1516, a daughter was born who survived infancy, the uneasiness was not altogether removed. She might marry a foreign prince and bring England under an alien yoke. Nor was the only precedent of a queen regnant encouraging; Matilda's reign had been a long unhappy succession of war and disorder. For a while Henry seems to have played with the notion of being succeeded by Henry Fitzroy, his son by Elizabeth Blount, a lady-in-waiting of the Queen; he created him Duke of Richmond at the age of six, with precedence over all dukes except any of the royal blood; but he must have realized that the English people were unlikely to accept a bastard for their king, and in any case Richmond died in 1536, a few

THE KING'S BUSINESS

weeks after witnessing the execution of Queen Anne.

When the years passed and still no child of Catherine survived except Mary, Henry's anxiety for an heir male was increased. It was not, however, until his passion for Anne Boleyn inflamed him that he came to the point of action. He discussed with his spiritual advisers the possibility of his marriage with Catherine being declared null and void *ab initio*, especially on the ground that Julius's dispensation had been *ultra vires*. There were recent precedents, even within his own family, for obtaining from Rome a divorce or, as it should be more properly described, a decree of nullity. The reigning Pope, Clement VII, who for a short while had enjoyed the revenues of the see of Worcester, would not be unfriendly and had granted similar requests. Henry's eldest sister Margaret, Queen Mother of Scotland, procured a divorce on 11th March, 1527, from the Earl of Angus, and soon after married Henry Stewart, who had divorced his wife. Henry professed to disapprove, and Wolsey wrote in his master's name reminding Margaret of "the divine ordinance of inseparable matrimony first instituted in Paradise," and protesting against "the shameless sentence sent from Rome." In the following year, Henry's brother-in-law, Charles Brandon, Duke of Suffolk, obtained from Clement VII a bull to protect his marriage with Henry's sister Mary, widow of Louis XII, from being invalidated because of his previous marriage with Margaret Mortimer who was still alive. Suffolk's complicated matrimonial record was as scandalous as Henry's was to become, and illustrates the contemporary disregard for the bond of matrimony by powerful princes and nobles. Francis I of France, like his predecessor Louis XII, had also obtained a divorce for very insufficient reasons. With such precedents Henry might hope for a favourable decision from Rome; but it was a highly inconvenient moment, as Catherine's nephew, the Emperor Charles V, had quarrelled with Clement VII, and a horde of Imperial troops—German, French and Italian—had lately sacked Rome and held the Pope virtually a prisoner. So for some time to come the Pope might find it his wisest policy to temporize.

Meanwhile, Henry had already begun to take steps. He had privately communicated his scruples to a few counsellors, and Wolsey summoned him to appear before Warham and himself, to justify his living with his brother's wife. The Cardinal, in view of his anti-Imperial policy of the moment, would have welcomed Henry's marriage to a daughter of Louis XII; it was not until a little later that he became aware of the King's intention to marry Anne. This was distasteful to Wolsey,

THE KING'S BUSINESS

but he conceived it his duty to promote "the King's business." Accordingly, in February, 1528, Stephen Gardiner and Edward Fox, Wolsey's secretaries and both of them soon to be bishops, were sent to Rome to obtain the appointment of a legatine commission to decide the King's case in England. They informed the Pope of the reasons of State for avoiding a disputed succession, and they went so far, in accordance with their instructions, as to threaten England's rupture with the Holy See if the King's will were thwarted. After prolonged negotiations Clement VII was prevailed upon to issue a commission for the King's suit to be tried in England by Cardinal Campeggio, who three years before had obtained by papal bull the bishopric of Salisbury, and by Cardinal Wolsey, *legatus a latere*. The terms of the commission were put in Campeggio's hands and not to be divulged, and he was privately advised to prevent the matter from coming to a trial by inducing the Queen to enter a nunnery or by dissuading the King from going further; if a trial proved unavoidable, Campeggio was instructed to defer sentence until he had communicated with Rome. The Pope thus hoped to guard himself against being committed to an unjust decision and exposing himself to the Emperor's anger. Campeggio, like the Pope, must play for time. He was actually seven months in England before the trial began. One excuse for the delay was that Catherine produced a copy of a Brief sent by Julius II to her mother in Spain, which professed to remedy any defects in his dispensation of 1503. Gardiner was sent again to Rome to discover the authenticity of the Brief, but, as it was not forthcoming, the Pope rightly refused to pronounce on its genuineness.

At last, on 31st May, 1529, the legatine court was formally opened in the great hall of the Black Friars, and the King and Queen were cited to appear on 18th June. Henry was represented by two proxies, but Catherine appeared in person, only to protest against the jurisdiction of the court. Her protest was registered but disallowed, and both she and Henry obeyed the summons to be present three days later. After Henry had stated his case, Catherine flung herself at his feet and implored him to bear in mind her helplessness as a foreigner, her dutifulness as a wife, and the honour of their daughter Mary. She made no further appearances and was pronounced contumacious (*i.e.*, disobedient to the court). After evidence had been taken about Arthur's marriage, and after much tedious discussion, Campeggio adjourned the court for the vacation usual at Rome, but it was generally recognized that it would not meet again. The legatine court had failed, and on 19th October, Wolsey resigned the Great Seal.

THE KING'S BUSINESS

Henry was naturally irritated by the prorogation of the court and the revoking of the case to Rome. Cranmer's secretary, Ralph Morice, narrates that the King came on 9th August to Waltham Abbey, and that Gardiner and Fox, who were now respectively the King's secretary and almoner, were billeted at the house of a Mr. Cressey, whose two sons were at the time being tutored there by Cranmer, they having left Cambridge because of an outbreak of plague. Cranmer was already "of old acquaintance" with Gardiner and Fox, who were heads of Cambridge colleges, and when they talked at supper about the King's business he urged that the lawfulness of marriage with a deceased brother's wife, in the light of Scripture, canon law and the Fathers, was a suitable question to be put to the universities. It is doubtful if Cranmer originated the idea, but it is certain that a few months later the King sent for him, instructed him to write a treatise on the matter, and quartered him on the Earl of Wiltshire, Anne's father. It is not true that Cranmer now became Anne's tutor—she was already twenty-two, and it is doubtful if she was living at home—but it was unseemly that he should be living under her father's roof when he was writing the treatise. Gardiner and Fox reported to the King in February, 1530, the measures they had been taking in Cambridge "to compass and attain your grace's purpose." The university was clearly unwilling to commit itself and it was only by means of what may be called a packed committee that a decision was reached, that Henry's marriage was illegal only if Arthur's marriage had been consummated (which Catherine was later to deny stoutly). Cambridge also avoided making any pronouncement on the right of Julius II to grant such a dispensation as he had made in 1503. Oxford showed even more reluctance until the King wrote two threatening letters, in one of which he bluntly said that it was not well to rouse hornets. Warham, Chancellor of Oxford, directed that, as the masters of arts were making difficulty, it would be better to remit the matter to a committee, and by a narrow majority the university agreed that the committee's decision should be regarded as the university's. Even this committee made the same reservation as Cambridge had done, so that the verdict was almost useless for the King's purpose, but he affected to regard it as negligible. Throughout the year 1530, the opinion of the continental universities was being canvassed, emissaries of the King being sent to procure, by any means including presents, favourable verdicts. The universities of France and Italy generally pronounced in a sense which the King could regard as favourable, but in Germany there was less success, the Lutherans especially taking their stand on the Levitical precept. The opinions thus collected might carry weight with the Pope, or, if he were still unaccommodating, they might furnish Henry with some apparent justification for acting independently of Rome.

Popular sympathy in England was clearly with Catherine, and her rival was frankly disliked. There was, however, some national resentment at a king of England being summoned to Rome, and his refusal to plead there in person was generally approved. The Queen refused to recognize any decision except that of Rome, and her patience was sorely tried by the Pope's delay, while Henry regarded this delay with increasing satisfaction as his chances of a favourable decision at Rome declined.

The King shrewdly fortified his position by securing the support of Parliament. At the beginning of 1532, an Act was passed, conditionally restraining the payment of annates and other dues to Rome, though leaving it to the King to put it into execution only if an amicable arrangement with the Pope could not be reached; the Act was a threat to spoliate the Papacy if Henry's wish for a declaration of nullity were not granted. The Act professed that "the King, and all his natural subjects, as well spiritual as temporal, be as obedient, devout, catholic, and humble children of God and Holy Church, as any people be within any realm christened." A year later, in February, 1533, a still more important Act was passed, restraining appeals to Rome and maintaining that all causes determinable by spiritual jurisdiction were to be decided in the King's courts, spiritual or temporal. This Act would enable Henry to have his suit determined in England without any reference to Rome. Both these Acts, with their far-reaching consequences for the relation of England with Rome, were passed before Cranmer had a voice in Parliament.

Cranmer was, indeed, out of the country in the King's service during the larger part of these years. In January, 1530, he was attached to the embassy of the Earl of Wiltshire to the Emperor; also attached was Stokesley, soon to be Bishop of London. Cranmer was with the Emperor when he met the Pope at Bologna. In Italy he used his influence to procure from the universities their judgments on the King's matrimonial business, and these he took to Rome, where he appears to have so far impressed the Pope that he was made Penitentiary for England. The embassy returned home in September. Again in January, 1532, Cranmer was appointed sole ambassador to the Emperor. Henry still retained some hope that Charles V might after all agree to his aunt's marriage being annulled; alternatively, it might be politic to keep in with the Lutheran princes so as to bring pressure on the Emperor. The time was not unfavourable because another formidable advance of the Turks towards Vienna obliged Charles to adopt a conciliatory policy to the princes whose help he needed. At Nuremberg, on 23rd July, 1532, he agreed that all suits against the Protestants should be dropped and peace was guaranteed until the next Diet or a General Council. The Nurembergers responded by contributing more than their quota to the Imperial army which was now assembling against the Turk. Cranmer also contrived to have an interview with John Frederick, who had just succeeded his father as Duke of Saxony and who was, like his father, a strong supporter of the Reformation. He made acquaintance for the first time with some of the Lutheran divines, especially Dr. Andreas Osiander, pastor of St. Laurence's church at Nuremberg. Although a priest, Cranmer married Osiander's niece, little dreaming what a handicap marriage would prove to be so soon afterwards when he was recalled by the King to fill the primatial throne at Canterbury. Public opinion might overlook Archbishop Wolsey having a mistress, but a married archbishop would be a more flagrant affront to traditional usage. But before that unexpected summons came, Cranmer had seen much of the preparations for the campaign against the Sultan. From Vienna he was posting two days behind the Emperor to rejoin him in Italy. From Villach, some ten miles distant from the Italian frontier, he sent to the King a graphic account of what he saw on the way. The Sultan seems to have thought better of his warlike intentions, and began to retreat, and the Imperial troops began to withdraw or desert. The Italian and Spanish soldiery which had crossed the Alps into Austria did not disperse without inflicting grievous damage on the Austrian villages and their inhabitants, and in retaliation the boors (peasants) "put no difference between one man and another, for all that go with the Emperor be to them Italians and Spaniards." Cranmer, making his journey in the Emperor's wake, writes that "these two days to come I shall be in more jeopardy of the boors than I was at any time yet." He tells of many Italians who, disgusted at the abandonment of the war and at the arrears of their pay, "chose captains among themselves and went before the Emperor, spoiling and robbing all the countries of Austria, Styria and Carinthia, as well churches as other houses, not leaving monstral (monstrance, receptacle for the Host) nor the sacrament." Even those with the Emperor behaved hardly any better:

> And the men of arms that come with the Emperor, and other that follow the court, do consume all that the other left, in such sort that

> I, following two days after the Emperor from Vienna, found in no town that was unwalled man, woman, nor child, meat, drink, nor bedding; but, thanked be God!, I found straw, hay and corn, for my horses to eat, and for myself and my servant to lie in, but the people were all fled into the mountains for fear.

Cranmer tells the King that he supposes the Emperor will treat of a General Council when he meets the Pope in Italy. Clement VII was nervous of a Council that might attempt to limit the papal autocracy as much as the Council of Basle had done. Rather than be confronted by a Council, he might be prepared to make concessions to the Protestants. Just before Emperor and Pope met in February, 1533, Cranmer left Mantua, where he was in attendance on the Emperor, for England. He had delayed his home-coming as long as he dared, hoping, as he said later, that the King "would be forgetful of me in the meantime." The diffident Cambridge scholar was reluctant to accept the primacy and it was Henry's habit to keep sees vacant for a year or more. Warham had died in the previous August and the Crown stood to gain by keeping sees unfilled, but the time was pressing. Anne was with child, and Henry secretly married her on or about 25th January, 1533, though Cranmer did not hear of it until about a fortnight later, nor was it generally known. At his trial at Oxford twenty-two years after, Cranmer hotly denied that there was any compact between him and the King—"Give me the archbishoprick of Canterbury, and I will give you licence to live in adultery"—but he must have realized that Henry intended him to decide the matrimonial issue, even if it should involve a rupture with Rome.

It was important to Henry that if the new primate was to decide his matrimonial cause there should be no technical defect in his consecration. He therefore pressed the Pope to expedite the sending of the necessary bulls authorizing the consecration. Henry was not yet excommunicated nor had the Pope pronounced on the marriage of Henry and Catherine. The King could still affect to be a dutiful son of the Church, and he ostentatiously took the papal Nuncio twice with him to Parliament. The consistory of cardinals were persuaded to approve the bulls, not without a hint being conveyed to them that the King might put into effect the Annates Act if the bulls were refused. The bulls were despatched with unusual celerity. Meanwhile, before Cranmer's arrival in England, the prior and convent of Canterbury had duly elected Thomas Cranmer to be archbishop. All was in order. On Passion Sunday, 30th March, 1533, immediately before the consecration in St. Stephen's, Westminster, the archbishop-elect read a protestation in the

Chapter House, in the presence of five ecclesiastical lawyers, who attested and signed the document. Long afterwards, at Cranmer's trial, the leading lawyer was to produce his full account, together with the protestation and the oaths taken on that day. Cranmer protested that in taking the customary oaths of allegiance to the Pope he interpreted them as a matter of form which must not dispense him from his supreme duty, his allegiance to the Pope obliging him only so far as it was consistent with his superior duty of obedience to the King. He counted himself still free to take counsel for the reform of religion, the governance of the Church of England and the prerogative of the Crown. Kneeling on the altar steps before taking the first oath to the Pope, he handed his protestation to the consecrating bishops, and after his consecration and before taking the second oath and receiving the pallium he repeated his protestation. In the second oath of allegiance to the Pope he inserted the phrase that has so often served to quiet the conscience of ecclesiastics—"saving my order" (*salvo meo ordine*). Last came the usual oath of allegiance to the King, which had always included a clause renouncing any grants from the Pope in the papal bulls that might be "hurtful or prejudicial to your Highness," but Cranmer added words that heightened its meaning. All the other bishops consecrated up to this time had taken similar oaths to the Pope and would soon be repudiating his jurisdiction, but probably none of them had taken that oath with the prospect of repudiation being so immediate. Some have sought to excuse Cranmer's protestation as arising from an honest scruple, but the more natural judgment is that it would have been more honourable for him to have informed the Pope through his proxy at Rome of the protestation he intended to make. At his trial the matter of the protestation told heavily against him and it was accounted perjury, but not a few of his judges had been untrue to their oath of allegiance to the Pope when Parliament and Convocation accepted the royal supremacy. Stephen Gardiner, who had taken the oath of fidelity to the Pope on becoming a bishop at the close of 1531, made a very similar exculpation three years later, when he signed the repudiation of papal jurisdiction and published his treatise *On True Obedience*.

On 10th May, the new archbishop opened his court at Dunstable Priory, in the neighbourhood of the Queen's temporary residence and pronounced her contumacious when she failed to answer his summons. Stokesley, Gardiner and two other bishops were assessors, and, though Cranmer must bear the chief responsibility, the others shared it with him. After thirteen days' examination of the evidence the archbishop gave his formal sentence that the marriage of Henry and Catherine was null and void, and, five days later, he pronounced Henry's marriage to Anne valid. Anne was crowned on Whit Sunday, in Westminster Abbey, and on 10th September, Cranmer stood godfather when Stokesley christened the Princess Elizabeth. Cranmer earned Henry's undying gratitude, but popular feeling was against the upstart Anne and in favour of the ill-used Catherine, half-Spanish though she was. When the "princess dowager of Wales," as Catherine was now styled, was moved from Ampthill to the Bishop of Lincoln's house at Buckden, in Huntingdonshire, she was acclaimed as Queen all along the road. In the face of many grievous humiliations and deprivations she passed her time in prayer and needlework, and, when one of her gentlewomen cursed Anne Boleyn, she said: "Curse her not, but pray for her; for the time will come shortly when you shall have much need to pity and lament her case." It was not until 23rd March, 1534, that the Pope pronounced her marriage with Henry to be valid, and, coming so late, the pronouncement could avail her nothing in worldly circumstance. On 7th January, 1536, she died, and on the 29th she was buried with much pomp in Peterborough Cathedral, although her daughter Mary was not allowed to be present. Four months later her rival was brought to the

CRANMER—THE ENGLISH REFORMATION

block. The long sordid story is only redeemed by Queen Catherine's honourable and dignified bearing, and, with larger reservations, by the union of Henry and Anne, which gave to England the most brilliant of her sovereigns.

Chapter Three

The Reformation Parliament
(1529-36)

PARLIAMENT was so closely associated with the Reformation, especially in the initial stages, that its record must be fully set out here, although two important Acts have already been mentioned in the previous chapters. For all his self-will, Henry VIII was astute enough to secure legal and parliamentary support for his most far-reaching designs. The most sweeping reforms and the widest extension of the royal prerogative could be enacted by Parliament, and the most unjust punishment of individuals, whether for treason or heresy, could be authorized by legal sentence. Henry was, indeed, a stickler for form; he was always more concerned to do legally than to do justly.

For the first twenty years of his reign Henry had been content to leave policy largely to his ministers, especially to Cardinal Wolsey, who as both *legatus a latere* and Lord Chancellor, exercised almost complete control of Church and State. Hitherto

CRANMER—THE ENGLISH REFORMATION

Henry had lived the life of a Renaissance prince with the occasional interruptions of a war or a diplomatic visit to the Continent. With Wolsey's fall in the autumn of 1529, the King, now in the thirty-ninth year of his age, took the reins into his own hands. The more he exerted his power, the more solid seemed the nature of that power. If the Pope would not do his will, he could defy him, and the sky would not fall or Emperor and French king combine to dethrone him. If the leading churchmen would not come to heel, he would intimidate them with the dread penalties of Præmunire and master the Church. He could induce Parliament to back him against the Church by appealing to the prejudices, grievances and greeds of its members. Henry was wiser than Wolsey in his relations with Parliament. In the fourteen years that Wolsey was Chancellor there had been only one Parliament, and he was unable to extract from it the whole of the grant he asked for, although he had gone in person to the House of Commons and so browbeaten its members that the Speaker, Thomas More, was driven to protest. By contrast, from the very morrow of Wolsey's fall, Henry looked to Parliament to further his designs. He has been called the greatest parliamentarian of all the English kings.

The most fateful of all English Parliaments, except perhaps the Long Parliament of Charles I's

THE REFORMATION PARLIAMENT

reign, was the Seven Years' Parliament that met on 3rd November, 1529, and, with several prorogations, continued till 1536. Hitherto Parliaments had seldom met for more than a few weeks before being prorogued or dissolved, and were not often continued into the following year. The Reformation Parliament did not sit continuously for long at a time; it met for some ten or eleven weeks in the winter months, and in the most eventful year, 1532, for a further session of four weeks in April and May.

The composition of the Upper House was very different from what it became soon after. There were only thirty-six lords temporal in the opening year of Henry VIII's reign, and their number was slightly increased by new creations later. The lords spiritual had a clear majority, as, besides the twenty-one diocesan bishops, there were twenty-six abbots and priors and one Master of an Order —forty-eight in a House of eighty-four. In the Lower House there were seventy-four county members and 222 burgesses; their number would be raised in 1543 to ninety, and 253 by the inclusion for the first time of representatives of Wales. It was usual for the Convocations of Canterbury and York to be summoned at the same time as Parliament; they still exercised their right and duty to tax the clergy for the King's needs and to pass canons or laws ecclesiastical, independently of King or Parliament. Henry found it easier to deal with the Church through Parliament than through Convocation, and bishops were obliged to discuss questions of church discipline and doctrine in the House of Lords as well as in Convocation.

The writs for the Parliament of 1529 were issued on 9th August, shortly after the prorogation of the legatine court and the revocation of Henry's suit to Rome. No one could doubt that the King would use Parliament to fortify himself at need against the likelihood of the Pope's refusal to pronounce the nullity of his marriage to Catherine. Before the opening of Parliament, the French ambassador, the Bishop of Bayonne, wrote home: "It is intended to hold a Parliament here this winter and act by their own absolute power, in default of justice being administered by the Pope in this divorce." It was also known that Parliament was expected to deal with ecclesiastical abuses or "enormities" as they were termed. In spite of these expectations, Henry was able to induce Sir Thomas More to accept the office of Lord Chancellor. He could count on More's strong sense of duty, but had to recognize his known opposition to the divorce by sparing him direct concern with that business. More, on his side, might adopt the advice he had given in *Utopia*: "That which you cannot turn to good, so to order

THE REFORMATION PARLIAMENT

it that it be not very bad." It was also significant of the laicizing of public life that Henry VIII should depart from precedent in appointing laymen to the offices of Chancellor and Privy Seal, and a little later should take another layman, Thomas Cromwell, for his principal secretary and eventually his Vice-Gerent. Henry may be regarded as the protagonist of the laity against the clergy, and he could count on the anti-clerical feeling prevalent in the House of Commons and among a large number of the temporal lords. That feeling had been revealed earlier in the reign and had little or no relation to any wish for doctrinal reform but was concerned with practical grievances. The insoluble question of the relations of Church and State which had troubled many reigns, including those of William I, Henry II and Edward I, had again become acute. Warham, just before his death at the age of eighty-two, had daringly remarked that the eighth Henry was going the way of the second and might meet the same fate; but there was no Becket now to withstand the King.

The new Chancellor opened Parliament with a speech in which, somewhat ungenerously as we might think, he described his predecessor as "the great wether which is of late fallen," and said that the King had marked him, "yea and saw through him, both within and without." More went on to indicate that "reform," of an undescribed nature, was to be the main business of this Parliament. Few observers could have guessed how far reform would be carried in this single Parliament—the rupture with Rome, the drastic curtailment of the constitutional rights of the Church, and the beginnings of the dissolution of the monastic houses. It is important, however, to notice that these severe reforms did not touch the Catholic faith except (and it is a big exception) so far as papal authority and the unity of the Church were concerned; these reforms might make the English Church schismatical, but not yet heretical.

Parliament proceeded to deal at once with various grievances, such as most churchmen would have admitted to be well founded. The laity were less concerned with complaints against papal jurisdiction than with the day-to-day administration by the Church Courts of all matters dealing with probate and matrimonial causes and discipline. Accordingly the Commons passed bills limiting the amount of fees payable for probate, burials and other dues. There was also a bill for reducing the evils of non-residence. Even these moderate reforms met with some opposition when the bills came before the Lords. Bishop Fisher took alarm at such reforms being initiated by the laity. "My Lords," he said, "you see daily what Bills come

THE REFORMATION PARLIAMENT

hither from the Common House, and all is to the destruction of the Church. For God's sake see what a realm the kingdom of Bohemia was; and when the Church went down, then fell the glory of the kingdom. Now with the Commons is nothing but 'Down with the Church!' And all this, me seemeth, is for lack of faith only." The Commons resented being called heretics in the Lords' chamber, and the Speaker conveyed their complaint to the King, who induced the bishop to explain his words and recommended a joint committee of selected members of both Houses, which accepted the bills in a modified form. Convocation naturally felt that the constitutional right of the Church to handle its own business was being taken out of its hands, although it was addressing itself to the removal of such abuses as the ordination of unfit persons and the neglect of parishes appropriated to monasteries. Wolsey's attempts at reform had been discountenanced by his own example of unparalleled pluralism and the scandal of his private life, but Warham's honest desire to improve the discipline of the Church could not be questioned. The Church was already being threatened with secular control, and if the King could carry Parliament with him, the Church, without the support of the Papacy, would be powerless to protect its ancient rights.

A still more serious threat to the Church's

independence arose next year. Soon after Wolsey died on 29th November, 1530, admitting that he had offended against the statute of Præmunire, the Attorney-General filed an injunction in the Court of King's Bench against the whole body of the clergy, for having laid themselves open to the extreme penalties of that Statute by having acknowledged Wolsey's legatine authority. It was no sufficient defence that the King himself had asked for Wolsey's appointment as legate and given him special licence to hold that commission. Præmunire was now a threat suspended over the heads of the clerical order, obliging them to take no action that was not covered by the approval of the King or by the King in Parliament. When Parliament and Convocation met again in the following January (1531), the latter body thought fit to buy immunity by proposing a grant of £40,000, and when it was intimated that this was not enough they raised their grant to over £100,000. Even then the King refused to accept this indemnity unless they would insert in their resolution a statement recognizing him as "Protector and Supreme Head of the English Church and Clergy." For three days the Upper House of Canterbury debated this unpalatable message. At last the aged Archbishop Warham proposed acceptance of the dangerous words with the addition of a saving clause—"as far as the law of

THE REFORMATION PARLIAMENT

Christ allows." The clause was almost valueless; who would have the legal right, King or Parliament or Convocation, to decide whether or not the law of Christ allowed this or that? The proposal found no seconder, and after a pause the archbishop said: "Whoever is silent means to consent." A voice said "Then we are all silent," and the clause was accepted by the Upper House, subsequently by the Lower House, and a little later by the Convocation of York, though not without a remonstrance from Tunstall, Bishop of Durham. Parliament embodied in a bill the King's pardon of the spiritualty, and also of the temporalty, for it, too, was liable to the penalties of Præmunire, though it secured exemption without a payment such as Convocation had made. It will be noted that there was as yet no explicit repudiation of papal jurisdiction nor any creation of a separate Church of England, but the way was prepared for the entire submission of the Church to the royal authority.

Considerable impetus to the process restricting the independence of the Church was given by the Petition of the Commons presented to the King on 18th March, 1532. Four drafts of it are extant with corrections in the hand of Thomas Cromwell, and it may well be that the Petition was initiated by him. Cromwell, like Gardiner, had been Wolsey's secretary before passing into the King's service, and he had recently been added to the Privy Council. In the next few years the direction of ecclesiastical affairs would increasingly fall into his hands, and his authority would overshadow that of the archbishop. The Petition begins by calling attention to the growth of "new fantastical and erroneous opinions," "contrary and against the very true Catholic and Christian faith," but complains of the conduct of the examinations for heresy in the Church courts. Supposed heretics are kept secretly in ward without bail, sometimes for a year or more. Subtle questions "concerning the high mysteries of our faith" are put to them such as are likely to "trap a simple, unlearned, or yet a well-witted layman without learning." If the Church courts condemn a man, he is delivered to the secular power "without remedy"; or, at best, he has to bear a faggot "to his extreme shame and undoing."

The petitioners complain of the power of Convocation to make ecclesiastical ordinances or canons "without your knowledge or most royal assent, and without the assent and consent of any of your lay subjects," although such canons, couched in Latin, may touch the person and property of laymen and also may be "to the diminution and derogation of your imperial jurisdiction and prerogative royal." They complain as well of the excessive fees and vexatious delays of the courts and of such burdens as the laity were only too prone to resent. A wrong is done, they say, to parishioners when the bishops appoint to a cure of souls those whom they call "their nephews or kinsfolk," sometimes while still infants.

The King passed the Petition to the archbishop, and an answer was drawn up by Gardiner, who had been given the see of Winchester a few months before. One passage concerning the archbishop's own courts is in Warham's name; he justly urges that a year ago Convocation had "reformed certain things objected here," and had taken other reforms in hand "within these ten weeks." As an old man "at the point to depart this world," Warham expresses the hope that the eminent services of learned doctors of civil law in the ecclesiastical courts may continue after his death. The Answer of the Ordinaries (i.e. bishops for the most part) admits that some Ordinaries have made mistakes and that minor officials, such as summoners, should be punished if they are found to be dishonest. As to persons being kept in ward before trial, it is "for sure custody" of "such as be suspected of heresy." There are happily few such but

> Truth it is that certain apostates, friars, monks, lewd (unlearned) priests, bankrupt merchants, vagabonds, and lewd idle fellows

of corrupt intent, have embraced the abominable and erroneous opinions lately sprung in Germany, and by them some seduced in simplicity and ignorance.

The bishops hold it to be their bounden duty to exercise their jurisdiction in dealing with heresy, and they stoutly maintain their ancient right to legislate for the Church without submitting such laws "to your highness's assent," but Convocation is willing to consider "your grace's mind and opinion" on any laws it shall propose. Gardiner, who was an able constitutionalist, argued that a continuance of ecclesiastical independence was compatible with acknowledging the royal supremacy; he hoped that by such cordial co-operation between Church and State there "shall ensue a most sure and perfect conjunction and agreement, as God being the chief corner-stone (*lapis angularis*) to agree and conjoin the same."

The King gave the Answer of the Ordinaries to the Speaker of the House of Commons with the comment: "We think this answer will scantly please you, for it seemeth to us very slender." In a second Answer the Ordinaries repeat their claim that the Church's jurisdiction was of Divine grant and not derived from the prince, but they offer a promise not to put forth any ordinance touching the laity without the King's consent.

THE REFORMATION PARLIAMENT

The upshot of the controversy was the Submission of the clergy, agreed by Convocation on 15th May, and delivered to the King by the archbishop the next day. Therein the clergy promised to promulgate no new canons without the King's licence and ratification and to submit any existing canons which "be thought to be not only much prejudicial to your prerogative royal, but also overmuch onerous to your highness's subjects" to the examination of sixteen "of the upper and nether house of the temporalty" and sixteen of the clergy, all to be chosen by the King. On the same day, 16th May, 1532, Sir Thomas More gave up the Great Seal, to the immense relief of his conscience, which had been sorely tried by the successive onslaughts on the ancient rights of the Church, and which was to be still more grievously strained, as he feared, by events soon to follow.

The King had obtained yet another formidable weapon with which to bring the Pope to terms— the Act for the conditional Restraint of Annates, passed in the first session of 1532. National feeling was easily stirred by the calculation that since the accession of Henry VII, £160,000 had passed "out of this realm unto the Court of Rome." The Act also provided that, if the bulls for the consecration of a bishop were deferred or refused, the archbishop of a province, with any other two bishops, was empowered to consecrate a person "named and presented by the King." Already also, before Cranmer became archbishop, Parliament had taken the most important step yet made against the Pope's authority in England. In February, 1533, it passed the Act for the Restraint of Appeals. The preamble was based on the political doctrine that "this realm of England is an empire," in the sense that it is a country whose sovereign owes no allegiance to any foreign superior. The Act opens with resounding phrases:

> Where by divers sundry old authentic histories and chronicles, it is manifestly declared and expressed, that this realm of England is an empire, and so hath been accepted in the world, governed by one supreme head and king, having the dignity and royal estate of the imperial crown of the same, etc.

It was pretended, in the usual English way, that no more was now being claimed than had been claimed "in the time of King Edward I, Edward III, Richard II, Henry IV, and other noble kings of this realm" against the encroachments of Rome in the "prerogatives, liberties and pre-eminences" of this realm and its jurisdiction. But there was one most important difference between the anti-papal statutes of previous reigns and this Act; those had sought to limit the papal jurisdiction, this Act abolished it altogether. The Act was also made retrospective, so that in particular, though it is not named, Catherine's appeal to Rome, and the King's suit which had been referred both to Rome and was still pending, were disallowed. It was a cowardly act to deprive Catherine of her right of appeal retrospectively.

This, then, was the general position when Cranmer became archbishop on 30th March, 1533. The papal jurisdiction was already abjured, but the rupture with Rome was not complete, and the King was armed with the support of Parliament and the helpless submission of the Clergy if he determined to go further. On the morrow of his consecration, Cranmer for the first time presided in Convocation, where for the previous three days the opinions of the universities on the divorce had been debated and Stokesley from the chair had ably advocated the King's case for the annulment of his marriage with Catherine, while Fisher led the opposition. A decision favourable to the King was reached, though in the face of a large minority. Armed with this limited support of Convocation, the archbishop could proceed to determine the issue between Henry and Catherine in his court at Dunstable.

Even at this stage Henry professed to be a dutiful son of the Church and obedient to the Holy Apostolic See in things lawful and honest, when on 29th June, 1533, he appealed from the Pope to a General Council and later obtained a declaration on the authority of Church Councils signed by several of the bishops. Henry would in fact, use or drop this appeal as it suited his turn at any particular moment. The Pope wrote a Brief declaring against Cranmer's pronouncement of the nullity of Henry's marriage with Catherine, but kept on postponing its publication. There was a disposition on both sides to avoid a final rupture; the door was left just ajar for an accommodation, but in the session of Parliament at the beginning of 1534, it was slammed with a series of Acts making the breach complete and irrevocable in Henry's reign. The Submission of the Clergy, accepted by Convocation two years before, was now made statutory, and without the saving clause. The restraint of the payment of annates to the Pope was now made absolute, and instead of their being abandoned as an intolerable burden they were to be paid to the Crown. When a see was vacant, the dean and chapter or, in a monastic cathedral, the prior and convent would continue to receive a *congé d'élire*, but along with it letters missive containing the name of the person nominated by the King; they must elect him or incur the penalties of Præmunire, and the bishop-elect was to be consecrated without procuring any bull from Rome. A further Act forbade the payment of Peter's Pence and authorized the archbishop to grant dispensations

THE REFORMATION PARLIAMENT

instead of the Pope. The Act declared that nothing in it should be interpreted as intending "to decline or vary from the congregation of Christ's Church in any things concerning the very articles of the Catholic faith of Christendom."

The last of the series of Acts passed in this spring session was the first Act of Succession. It asserts it to be the ancient right of "emperors, kings and princes" to decide the succession without interference of "the Bishop of Rome" or "other foreign princes." The marriage with "the Lady Katherine" is declared null and Anne's marriage to be "good and consonant to God's law" and her issue legitimate and heritable. If any persons "maliciously" deny the King's title, they shall be "adjudged high traitors." All nobles, both spiritual and temporal, and any other subjects of whom it shall be required, shall take an oath to maintain the contents of the Act. No form of oath was included in the Act, but before Parliament was prorogued a form was supplied by letters patent, and this oath, with unimportant differences, was included in the second Act of Succession, passed in the following November. On the day that Parliament was prorogued, 30th March, 1534, the members of both Houses took the oath. It is surprising that it was not refused by any then present, including the bishops. A commission was appointed to administer the oath, consisting of the archbishop, Audley the Lord Chancellor, Cromwell and the Abbot of Westminster. The first to be summoned before them on 13th April, were Fisher and More. Fisher had already been sentenced to imprisonment (though the sentence was remitted) for his alleged collusion with the so-called Nun of Kent, who had foretold Henry's perdition for marrying Anne. Thomas More, since resigning the chancellorship, had lived quietly at home, scrupulously avoiding any political utterances. Both men were willing to swear to the succession, as they recognized the right of the King and Parliament to determine it and the subject's duty of obedience to lawful authority, but they had scruples about the particular form of the oath, which, by including an obligation to maintain "all the whole contents and effects" of the Act, would commit them to a declaration of Mary's illegitimacy and a repudiation of the Pope's authority. As they refused the actual oath prescribed, the commissioners could only act according to their instructions, but four days later Cranmer wrote to Cromwell, strongly urging that it would be enough to accept such an oath to maintain the succession as "the Bishop of Rochester and Master More" were willing to take. It would be "a good quietation to many other within this realm" if it were known that these men accepted the succession, and the exact terms allowed to them need not be published. But the King was obdurate, and the two men were confined in the Tower until fresh proceedings were brought against them after more than a year. In prison, More wrote his *Dialogue of Comfort against Tribulation* and other deeply religious treatises in the beautiful English of which he was master. But this abstinence from all religious or political controversy would not save him or his fellow-prisoner. A severe Treasons Act was passed in November, 1534, which made it high treason from the 1st February next to deny the King any of his titles, including that of Supreme Head. More and Fisher were included in an Act of Attainder for misprision of treason (a misdemeanour akin to treason, liable to perpetual imprisonment and forfeiture of goods but not to death). The King and Cromwell would probably have been pleased to procure the submission of two men so widely respected as the bishop and the late Lord Chancellor, and Cromwell and others visited More in the Tower and used persuasive words and manner as well as threats, but without avail. Fisher's chance of life was not improved when the news came that Paul III had made him a cardinal. The King is said to have remarked: "Well, let the Pope send him a hat when he will; but I will provide that whensoever it cometh, he shall wear it on his shoulders, for head he shall have none to set it on." On 22nd June, 1535, after being condemned as a traitor, Fisher was brought to the scaffold on Tower Hill, and when the sun shone full in his face, he quoted in Latin a verse of the 33rd Psalm: "Look unto Him and be illumined, and your faces shall not be confounded."

Ten days later, More was brought for trial before a special commission, entirely of lay persons, the archbishop having no part in it. He still declined the oath of succession, but refused to give his reasons. As for the royal supremacy, he neither affirmed or denied it, but his silence, instead of being taken as consent, was interpreted as denial. Nor was it of any avail for him to urge that the severe Treasons Act limited verbal treason to what was said "maliciously." After the sentence of "guilty" was pronounced, Audley, his successor as Lord Chancellor, asked him why he had refused what "the bishops, universities, and best learned of this realm" had accepted. More made the truly Catholic answer, that if the bishops of Christendom of the present age and of all the Christian centuries be considered, he was in no minority:

> And therefore am I not bounden, my Lord, to conform my conscience to the Council of one realm against the general Council of Christendom. For of the foresaid holy bishops

> I have, for every bishop of yours, above one hundred; and for one Council or Parliament of yours (God knoweth what manner of one), I have all the Councils made these thousand years. And for this one kingdom, I have all other Christian realms.

Thomas More, unsupported by the English bishops save Fisher, or by any of the prominent orthodox laymen, stood for the unity of Christendom, while his royal master and his ministers, both spiritual and temporal, stood for the unity of the nation. There could be no compromise on either side. More's characteristic humour did not desert him at the end; when he mounted the scaffold, as his son-in-law Roper tells, he said: "I pray you, Master Lieutenant, see me safe up, and for my coming down let me shift for myself." Holbein has drawn for us the spiritual and ascetic face of John Fisher as well as the portraits of Thomas More and his family; they are in marked contrast with his portraits of many of Henry's courtiers, which reveal their greed and unscrupulous ambition.

Just as the Succession Act was the undoing of More and Fisher, so the Supremacy Act cost the lives of other sincere men. This Act, designating the King to be "the only supreme head in earth of the Church of England" passed in November, 1534, did not, indeed, prescribe penalties, but the Treasons Act, passed later in the same session, made it a capital offence to deny "maliciously" the King's titles. For refusing to recognize Henry as Supreme Head, the most learned monk in England, Dr. Richard Reynolds, head of the Brigittine monastery of Sion, and the prior of the London Charterhouse, together with two other Carthusian priors, were brought before a tribunal of judges and lay peers. The jury could not agree to find them guilty, because it was conscience, not malice, that had moved them to refuse the title. The judges told the jury that the word was superfluous and that any denial was malicious. Still they held out until Cromwell threatened them into giving an adverse verdict, and the men were condemned to death. Cranmer, who had had no part in their trial, at once wrote to Cromwell, pleading for Reynolds, for whose learning and character he had much respect, and for the prior of Axholme. "If there be," he wrote, "none other offence laid against them than this one, it will be much more for the conversion of all the fautors thereof, after mine opinion, that their consciences may be clearly averted" by persuading them to another view; "and if it would please the King's highness to send them unto me, I suppose I could do very much with them in this behalf." But this appeal for more merciful and sensible treatment, like so many

THE REFORMATION PARLIAMENT

other appeals of Cranmer's, fell on deaf ears. Reynolds, on being asked by the Chancellor why he refused what had been accepted by the bishops and lords in Parliament, answered: "I am sure the larger part of the kingdom is at heart of our opinion, although outwardly, partly from fear, partly from hope, they profess to be of yours." A few weeks before Fisher was executed, the four monks were hanged at Tyburn in their monastic habits—for which there was no precedent—with attendant circumstances of unspeakable barbarity.

Before the Seven Years' Parliament dissolved there was still one great matter to handle. In February, 1536, it received a digest of the reports of the visitors appointed to inspect the monasteries, and it proceeded to pass the first Act for the Dissolution. The importance of this Act demands treatment in a separate chapter.

It remains to assess Cranmer's responsibility for any of the Acts passed by the Reformation Parliament from the time that he first entered the House of Lords. Within a few days of his consecration, Parliament was prorogued, so that his effective membership begins only with the spring session of 1534, which passed a series of important Acts, including the Submission of the Clergy (already accepted by Convocation before Cranmer became archbishop), the Restraint of Appeals

CRANMER—THE ENGLISH REFORMATION

(adopted by Parliament in 1532, but now made absolute) and the first Act of Succession. There is no doubt that he welcomed the succession being assigned by law to the issue of Henry and Anne. The terminating of the papal jurisdiction, effected by the prohibition of appeals to Rome and of payments of Peter's Pence and other customary dues, would have met with his full approval. As he tells the King in a letter of 1536:

> "I perceived the see of Rome work so many things contrary to God's honour and the wealth (well-being) of this realm, and I saw no hope of amendment so long as that see reigned over us; and for this cause only I had prayed unto God continually, that we might be separated from that see; and for no private malice or displeasure that I had either to the bishop or see of Rome."

He allows that some of the Pope's laws are "good and laudable," though they are not to be reckoned "equal with God's law," and their observance does not entitle a man to remission of sins; but he points out that those that are good are still "received as the law of the realm" and should be observed. So, too, with many ceremonies of the Church which are still retained: the bare observance of them is not "in itself a holiness before God," but "they be a remembrance of holy things, or a disposition unto holiness."

Cranmer also upheld the royal supremacy and

THE REFORMATION PARLIAMENT

assiduously preached it throughout his diocese and especially in "mine own church of Canterbury," where it met with some opposition. He sincerely believed that the Crown was more likely than Convocation to promote the needed reform of the Church. In Convocation the reforming bishops were in a minority throughout Henry's reign and met with strenuous opposition, but the archbishop could generally count on the King's support. He disliked lawlessness and sought to restrain the clergy from contentious preaching when they were all too ready to preach for or against the marriage with Anne. No doubt he welcomed the Act for the provision of suffragan bishops, and perhaps drew up its details. On the other hand, it is unlikely that he was easy in mind about the severe penalties prescribed by the Treasons Act, and certainly he repeatedly sought to save those who incurred those penalties.

Chapter Four

The Dissolution of the Monasteries

ONE clause of the Act forbidding the payment of Peter's Pence had had an ominous sound; the archbishop should have no authority to visit monasteries or other religious houses previously exempt from episcopal supervision, but such supervision should be exercised by the King or by those whom he commissioned under the Great Seal. The way was thus prepared for the Dissolution without the interference of the bishops or other Church authorities. By the Act of Supremacy the King was given authority to "visit, repress, redress, reform, order, correct, restrain and amend" all errors, heresies and abuses. Henry had thus secured parliamentary sanction for a drastic handling of the monastic and diocesan life of the Church, its property (and even its doctrine) by the King or those whom he commissioned to act. The full danger of this royal absolutism became apparent when the King delegated his spiritual jurisdiction to his principal secretary, whom at the beginning of 1535 he appointed Vicar-General or Vice-Gerent in all causes ecclesiastical. It was a grievous limitation of the primate's authority. If Cromwell, in fulfilment of a commission dated 21st January, 1535, was to hold a visitation of churches, clergy and monasteries, the constitutional rights and duty of the provincial archbishop and of the diocesan bishops to visit were suspended. In particular, the whole business of preparing for the dissolution of the monasteries was committed to Cromwell and the visitors he appointed, while the archbishops and bishops were powerless. Cromwell, as a result of hasty visits by himself and his subordinates, prepared a damning report to Parliament or "Comperta" of the abuses he proposed to find, and that report influenced Parliament in passing in 1536 the Act for the dissolution of all monasteries with an annual income of less than £200.

The suppression of particular monasteries for their alleged uselessness was no new thing. Before the Reformation, Wolsey had, as we have seen, suppressed several of the smaller ones, using Cromwell as his principal agent. Now that the rupture had come with Rome, and the King and Cromwell were vested with unlimited powers, it was possible to take wholesale measures. It was easier to make a case against the smaller houses, some of which were less than half full and in financial distress, nor had they as powerful friends as the great and famous houses; it is possible, too, that the smaller houses suffered more than the larger from lax discipline. It is not, however, conceivable that so hasty a visitation as Cromwell and his colleagues made afforded the means of making a just assessment of their relative merits and demerits. Cromwell, instigated less by religious or moral concern than by a desire to enrich his master, and incidentally himself, intended to find an adverse judgment.

There is also no doubt that the covetous eyes of many laymen were cast on the monastic properties. By the Act all monasteries of an annual value less than £200 were suppressed and their properties given to the King and his heirs, "to do and use therewith his and their own wills, to the pleasure of Almighty God and to the honour and profit of this realm." As might be expected of the land-owning members of the Houses of Parliament, they safeguarded their rights as holders or stewards of monastic property. Even before the Act was passed many monasteries had surrendered, and the surrenders were legalized by the Act. By the Act 376 monastic houses were dissolved, though some purchased an uneasy, and, as it proved, very short respite.

In many parts of the country the dissolution was viewed with apathy or with little sympathy, but in Lincolnshire and the North there was at once an explosion of resentment. A sudden rising

DISSOLUTION OF THE MONASTERIES

in Lincolnshire was broken up without much difficulty by troops under the Duke of Suffolk. The petitioners, in professing loyalty to the King, asked that he should remove from his Council such upstarts as Cromwell and Cranmer, but they only drew upon them Henry's angry words, reported to them by the Lancaster Herald:

> Rude commons of a most brute and beastly shire, how should ye presume to find fault with your Prince for the election of his councillors and prelates? Ye call yourselves true subjects, but ye are foul traitors. Ye speak of the suppression of the religious houses: but the religious houses were given to us by Act of Parliament: none are suppressed where God was well served, but those where most vice, mischief, and abomination of living were used.

A far more serious rising, beginning in Lincolnshire and spreading to Yorkshire and the North, under the name of the Pilgrimage of Grace, was started by many noblemen, gentry, abbots and parish priests. Their chief grievance was the suppression of the monasteries, but they demanded also the extirpation of heresy, the legitimizing of the Lady Mary and the dismissal of Cromwell, Audley and others. (Social grievances here, as also in Lincolnshire, were mentioned—high taxes, enclosures, rack-rents, rising prices and so on.) The leaders, besides many of their humbler followers, were punished with death. So far from saving the smaller monasteries, the rising only gave an excuse for going on to the complete destruction of all. Some of the abbots of northern houses were implicated in the rising—voluntarily or involuntarily, there was no sufficient enquiry to determine which—and paid for it by being hanged at their own gates, as were the abbots of Whalley and Sawley. The abbots of Fountains and Jervaulx were also condemned to death. Another abbot saved his skin by surrendering his monastery, and in the next three years several other houses surrendered, sometimes by the abbot or prior making terms for himself, or even by an abbot being newly appointed with a corrupt undertaking that he should surrender his house.

The Act of 1536 had stated that monks and nuns of suppressed houses, if they wished to remain "religious" should be "committed to great and honourable monasteries," there "to live religiously, for reformation of their lives"; for the Act hypocritically avers that there were "great solemn monasteries of this realm wherein (thanks be to God) religion is right well kept and observed." This testimony to the excellent conduct of some of the greater monasteries did not save them. One of the first measures of the new Parliament of 1539 was an Act to suppress all the remaining monasteries and to vest their posses-

DISSOLUTION OF THE MONASTERIES

sions in the Crown. Cromwell, with his long experience as secretary in turn of Wolsey and Henry VIII, knew well how to compile complete inventories of monastic property, and he achieved his purpose of enriching his royal master.

It would have been well that at least some large proportion of the monastic properties had been assigned to the needs of the Church, education and other public charitable purposes; a great opportunity was missed. Hugh Latimer, Bishop of Worcester, tried to save Malvern Priory for educational use, but did not succeed. Six new bishoprics indeed were founded, though one of them, Westminster, was short-lived. In general, the spoils went to the Crown at its absolute discretion. Some gifts of land were made to courtiers and were the foundation of great families; more often, laymen obtained lands by purchase or lease from the Crown. A few of the great monastic churches were saved from destruction by being established as the cathedrals of the new bishoprics, or by the citizens acquiring them, generally by purchase, for use as parish churches, as at Tewkesbury, Sherborne and St. Albans: but the far larger number were despoiled and suffered to go to ruin, or their stones were quarried, with permission or without, for the building of private residences and farm buildings. The loss to the country of such noble fanes as Fountains, Furness,

Tintern, Evesham and Bury St. Edmunds, cannot be measured, and their precious contents were commonly destroyed, or passed insecurely into private hands and have since largely disappeared.

It may be asked, what degree of responsibility had the Archbishop of Canterbury for all this wasteful destruction? "Of all the great movements affecting the Church," says James Gairdner, "Cranmer had least to do with the suppression of the monasteries." By the Act of 1534 forbidding papal dispensations the archbishop was expressly deterred from any right to visit monasteries; this was the sole right of the King, who might exercise it through any whom he commissioned. Cromwell and his subordinates, and various other commissioners, alone handled the monastic business from start to finish; the archbishop was only a passive spectator. Even in Convocation the Vicar-General or his deputy presided, and Injunctions to the clergy were issued by Cromwell in the King's name. There seems to have been an uneasiness in Cranmer's mind when he wrote to Cromwell on 22nd April, 1536, when the dissolution of the smaller monasteries was beginning:

> I was ever hitherto cold, but now I am in a heat with the cause of religion, which goeth all contrary to mine expectation, if it be as the fame goeth; wherein I would wonder fain break my mind unto you, and if you please I will

DISSOLUTION OF THE MONASTERIES

come to such place as you shall appoint for the same purpose.

But we do not know if Cranmer's plea had any effect. Both he and Latimer approved of the removal of objects of superstition—as they esteemed them—from cathedral and parish churches, and the archbishop desired any changes to be effected with the authority of law and not by unauthorized acts of violence. Cranmer appears to have viewed with satisfaction the conversion of the cathedral priory of Christ Church, Canterbury, to a new foundation of dean and chapter, though it brought him also much ill-will and opposition. On one important point he made a wise and successful protest. When Lord Chancellor Rich, the King's attorney and other commissioners were framing the regulations for the school on the Canterbury foundation, some of the commissioners were for admitting gentlemen's sons only to the school.

Whereunto that most reverend father, Thomas Cranmer, Archbishop of Canterbury, being of a contrary mind, said that he thought it not indifferent so to order the matter. For (said he) poor men's children are many times endued with more singular gifts of nature, which are also the gifts of God, as with eloquence, memory, apt pronunciation, sobriety, with such like, and also commonly more given to apply their study, than is the gentleman's son delicately educated.

We may also ask how far the changes were acceptable to clergy and people or were resented. The answers can be only provisional as the evidence is incomplete and will be differently assessed by those (to-day or in any other day) who are disposed to justify the changes and by those who believe them to have been largely uncalled for. The repudiation of papal jurisdiction and the substitution, in large part, of royal in place of papal authority excited less comment than might have been expected. Actual resistance to the King's will was highly dangerous. Warham would often repeat "the wrath of the King is as messengers of death" (*Ira principis mors est*, Proverbs XVI. 14), and others after him echoed it with further experience of its truth. There were few in high places who, like More and Fisher, would court death. Yet even the strong-willed Tudor monarch could not have got his way if he had not found statesmen and Parliament ready, if sometimes reluctantly, to approve his ecclesiastical policy, and a people acquiescent, if also not easily convinced. The rupture with Rome was to many distressing, but they might readily hope it was only temporary; kings, both English and continental, before the Reformation had brought upon themselves interdict and excommunication, and yet had before long effected a reconciliation. And the rupture came when the rising national temper was less willing to put up with papal exactions or the protracted delays of the Pope and the Curia.

Chapter Five

The Royal Supremacy

THE Royal Supremacy was harder to accept. The King might seek to assure those who boggled at it that it did not extend to strictly spiritual functions, and only time would show how far he crossed the border-line. Since Henry constantly professed his adherence to the Catholic faith and repressed heresy, some of the conservative bishops might even believe that he would prove the best upholder of the faith, now that the support of the Papacy was gone. The most orthodox bishops—Stokesley, Tunstall, Gardiner—accepted the Royal Supremacy, and Gardiner became its ablest advocate in his *De Vera Obedientia* (1535). Both he and Cranmer, from different angles, would find the weakness of the theory later—Gardiner when the Supremacy was exercised by the ministers of Edward VI in his minority, and Cranmer when at the beginning of her reign Mary, too, was able to make religious

THE ROYAL SUPREMACY

changes through being Supreme Head. It was an awkward predicament for Gardiner when in Mary's reign an English translation of his *On True Obedience* was widely circulated in England and quoted by a heretic on trial before him.

The average Englishman has seldom been much concerned about theories, but he is apt to resent interference with his use and wont. The spoliation of his parish church, its images and shrines, its silver ornaments and rich silk apparels, would offend him more than any doctrine about the Supremacy and papal authority. These things touched his religious life at a tender spot where he might well think he had the right to retain what was endeared to him by long and reverent associations. A London crowd might be diverted by the burning on the steps of St. Paul's of a wonder-working image fetched up from Boxley or Worcester, but it was quite another thing to see your parish church robbed of its familiar features. There was some deliberate looting and some violent unauthorized iconoclasm; such acts were "popular" in the sense that they were impromptu, but they would almost certainly have shocked the ordinary quiet parishioner.

Henry VIII's profession of orthodoxy was not merely politic, though it was that, but also it represented his mind. As a young man he had been punctilious in his church observances and he continued to the end of life to practise them. The Defender of the Faith had won fame by crossing swords with Luther and he continued to suppress heresy. He might find it politic at times to court the German Protestant princes and correspond with Lutheran divines, but they rightly mistrusted his pretended sympathy with them, and he would quickly drop them if the change of circumstances allowed him to do so safely. Heretics received short shrift, with the support of Parliament which often urged the extirpation of heresy.

Thomas Bilney, a gentle soul, if also erratic and without any worldly wisdom, was one of the first to be burnt, a year and a half before Cranmer became archbishop; he had preached against the mediation of the saints, but in most respects he was orthodox. A more interesting case is that of John Frith, who was accused of denying purgatory and transubstantiation. By the King's orders he was examined by the Lord Chancellor, Suffolk, the Earl of Wiltshire, Cranmer, and Bishops Stokesley and Gardiner. The archbishop sought to persuade him but could not move him. His case was then remitted to Stokesley, Gardiner and the Bishop of Chichester; Stokesley condemned him as an obstinate heretic, he was handed over to the secular arm, and burnt at Smithfield, on 4th July, 1533. He has been called "the most genuine martyr of the English Reformation," because "he died to establish the difference between a necessary article of faith and a thing which may be left indifferent." If the Reformation had meant freedom of conscience this description would be accurate. With real largeness of mind he was willing to allow that his opponents were right in their opinions and he claimed only liberty of conscience to think otherwise. In the Articles which he drew up as he awaited death, he wrote:

> Though this opinion were indeed true (which thing they can neither prove true by Scripture nor doctors) yet could I not in conscience grant that it should be an article of the faith necessary to be believed: for there are many verities which yet may be no such articles of our faith. It is true that I lay in irons when I wrote this; howbeit I would not have you to receive this truth for an article of our faith; for ye may think the contrary without all jeopardy of damnation.

In the next year thirteen obscure anabaptists, whose very names are unrecorded, were burnt.

In the years that follow the Reformation Parliament we can detect the constant tension between rival parties in the Church. There were those who would carry the Reformation further than the breach with Rome and the mending of certain abuses, chiefly financial; and there were those, of whom Gardiner was the leader, generally with the support of Tunstall and Bonner, who, while accepting the Royal Supremacy and the repudiation of the Papacy, were chiefly concerned to prevent the English Church from being contaminated by Lutheran opinions and practices. It was a long-drawn and fairly even struggle between reformers and conservatives. The reform movement was a good deal discredited by the wild utterances in pulpit and press of the more fanatical men and by popular acts of iconoclasm and irreverence which shocked and alarmed those to whom the ancient pieties were still dear. The Convocation which met in June, 1536, a few weeks after Anne Boleyn's execution, under the presidency of Cromwell's deputy, Dr. Peter, was bound to deal with the disorder and confusion that threatened the Church, and it adopted the Ten Articles, whose express purpose was "to stablish Christian quietness and unity among us, and to avoid contentious opinions." These Articles represent something of a compromise between old and new opinions, with the balance slightly in favour of the former. The orthodox view of the Scriptures was stated without use of the word "transubstantiation," auricular confession was upheld as "a very expedient and necessary mean" and, although justification is by faith and for Christ's merits and not man's, there is the characteristically English proviso that "it is our necessary duty to do good works." A distinction is made between these necessary articles of faith and the argument which follows for the retention of certain customary uses and "laudable ceremonies"; images, "the kindlers and stirrers of men's minds," are retained, but superstitious use of them is to be abandoned; men may pray to the saints to intercede for them, though it must not be supposed that "any saint is more merciful or will hear us sooner than Christ"; charity requires that we should pray for souls departed, but since Scripture is uncertain about the name of the place where they are and the "kind of pains there," we must "refer the rest wholly to God, to whom is known their estate and condition." The old customs of holy water, the bearing of candles on Candlemas Day, palm on Palm Sunday, and ashes on Ash Wednesday, and "creeping to the Cross" on Good Friday, are to be retained "to put us in remembrance of those spiritual things that they do signify." Two months later Royal Injunctions were issued by the authority of Cromwell as Vice-Gerent, though probably with Cranmer's approval, as he was concerned with the maintenance of order. According to these Injunctions the Ten Articles are to be expounded in sermons distinguishing between what is "necessary to be holden and believed for our salvation" and "ceremonies, rights and usages of the Church meet and convenient to be kept." Images and relics are not to be made matter of gain (lucre), and it is better to bestow money on the relief of the poor than to spend it in the adornment of images or on pilgrimages. Parsons are to see that the young are taught the Lord's Prayer, the Creed and the Ten Commandments in their mother tongue. They are to reside in their cures, give themselves to the study of the Bible, and for every hundred pounds of their stipend they are to maintain an exhibitioner at Oxford or Cambridge. This last provision would have been specially welcome to Cranmer and Latimer who deplored the threatened decay of the universities. Other Injunctions in 1538 went a stage further; they ordered not only that children should learn the Paternoster and Creed in English, but that priests should see that all who came to confession in Lent could recite them. Lighted candles were to be allowed only "before the Sacrament of the altar," the rood, and the Easter sepulchre. No alterations in the prescribed services, which were still those of the Sarum use in Latin, were allowed until they should have been authorized, except only that the commemoration of Thomas Becket was to be abandoned forthwith. Most important of all, in Cranmer's judgment, was the order that a copy of the English Bible (the Great Bible), soon to be published, was to be placed in every church so that it could conveniently be read by the parishioners; of this feature of the English Reformation more will be said later.

A further example of compromise between reformers and conservatives is seen in the *Institution of a Christian Man*, of 1537, commonly known as the Bishops' Book, because it was chiefly drawn up by Cranmer and Bishop Fox of Hereford and received the assent of all the bishops; it was issued with the King's permission but without any such commendatory preface as he had prefixed to the Ten Articles. There were prolonged and embittered discussions in composing the *Institution*. Latimer at one stage of the controversy wrote to Cromwell: "For my part, I had lever be poor parson of poor Kynton again than to continue thus bishop of Worcester," but towards the end he was surprised and heartened by agreement being reached. The *Institution* was more evenly balanced than the Articles; it might be hoped, too, that Catholics would be pleased to see the recognition as sacraments of four which had not been named in the Articles—confirmation, matrimony, holy orders, and extreme unction, while Protestants would welcome the teaching on justification by faith, though it would not have satisfied German Lutherans.

So far, then, the balance had been kept fairly even, but it would be entirely turned towards reaction in the Six Articles of June, 1539. For some months a committee, appointed by Parliament, of bishops representing the old and the new views had been vainly seeking agreement upon a statement of doctrine; and the Duke of Norfolk, commenting on this failure, introduced in the House of Lords on 16th May, 1539, the statute of the Six Articles, which uncompromisingly insisted upon transubstantiation, communion in one kind only as necessary, clerical celibacy, inviolable vows of chastity, private masses and compulsory auricular confessions. Denial of transubstantiation was heresy punishable with death; and denial of the other five articles was felony and might mean a felon's death. The bishops in the House of Lords debated the Bill while the temporal peers sat silent. For three days Cranmer contended against it, but he, and all those bishops who supported him except Shaxton, yielded when the King came to Parliament in person and urged the passing of the measure. Cranmer's only defence, long years after, was his conception of the duty that he owed to the King. It was a defence that could hardly have satisfied his own conscience. Ought he to have resigned his see, as Latimer did at once? He was never an ambitious man, and for his own happiness would always have preferred the scholar's quiet life, but he may have judged that his retirement would leave the field to his opponents, whereas the King might again veer round to the support of reformation. He had not yet abandoned the orthodox belief about the Eucharist.

The savage penalties of the Six Articles were exacted freely in the next twelvemonth though after that they were much less often used. The same Parliament which had adopted the Act of the Six Articles also completed the destruction of the monasteries and upheld the Royal Supremacy. On 30th July, 1540, three priests, condemned by an act of attainder for denying the Supremacy, were executed as traitors, while Dr. Barnes and two other preachers were burnt as heretics.

This time of brutal reaction was viewed with dismay by the German Protestants, who had been hoping to see the Reformation well launched in England under Henry VIII. English envoys, including Bishop Day and Heath, the future archbishop of York, had been despatched, with a friendly greeting from the King, to the Diet of the Schmalkaldic League, in 1535. The Leaguers were willing to accept King Henry as their patron, if he would assent to the Augsburg Confession. Bishop Gardiner, then our ambassador in France, warned the King against compromising his orthodoxy and his position as Supreme Head by any doctrinal agreement with the Protestants abroad, but Henry was willing that conferences should continue. After three months' conference at

Wittenberg (15th January to 24th April, 1536), the English envoys came home with nothing effected. Two years later, when there seemed to be likelihood of continental war, Henry made fresh overtures, as a result of which three German delegates arrived in England on 12th May, 1538, and were soon in discussion with a small group of bishops, including Cranmer and Tunstall. Cranmer entertained them at Lambeth and would certainly have been glad to reach an understanding. They reached a fairly close agreement on doctrinal matters, but as to the alleged "abuses"—communion in one kind, celibacy, private propitiatory masses—the King himself expressed his unwillingness to give in to the Lutherans. In the previous November Henry had himself presided at the trial of John Lambert, who had consorted with Lutherans in Germany, and he announced: "I will be no patron of heretics." The Lutherans, on their part, were willing to make many concessions in order to get England's concurrence. They would accept Episcopacy, leave freedom to other churches to continue communion in one kind, and retain some monasteries if they were kept up to the mark and if some were devoted to educational purposes; but they insisted on the abolition of "abuses." After staying nearly a year, they returned empty-handed. The passing of the Six Articles seemed to destroy their last hope,

THE ROYAL SUPREMACY

though Melancthon, a man with great conciliatory gifts, wrote to Henry believing or affecting to believe that the act was due to the bishops and against the King's wishes.

The German hopes were revived when Cromwell promoted the marriage of the King, to Anne, daughter of the Lutheran Duke of Cleves, but that marriage foundered at once and was the occasion of Cromwell's downfall. The danger, if it ever existed, of the Emperor's making war on Henry was past, and alliance with the Protestant princes was no longer needed. There would be only one other attempt, in 1544, to reach an understanding between the German Protestants and England, and by that time the chances of agreement were even less.

Cromwell's blunder over the Anne of Cleves marriage, besides his favouring a Protestant alliance, gave Gardiner the looked-for opportunity of procuring his dismissal. By a bill of attainder on the charge of treason, passed without the accused being allowed to defend himself, Cromwell was brought to the block on 28th July, 1540. He had used the same method to destroy his enemies. Before the second reading of the bill Cranmer had the courage to plead for him with the King, but, like most of his many pleas for mercy, it was unavailing. It may be doubted whether Cromwell had any religious principles; it was for his own ends and for the King's enrichment that he destroyed the monasteries and intimidated the clergy. On the scaffold, he said: "I die for the Catholic Faith of Holy Church," but it did not save him or deserve to save him. He had, no doubt, by his masterful control as Vice-Gerent, advanced the cause of the Reformation in England, but his enemies were strong enough to compass his downfall.

Many were ready to wager that Cranmer would follow Cromwell to the Tower, and many desired it, for the cause of the Reformation was still the cause of a minority. Could that cause survive, now that Cromwell had gone? Had Cranmer the requisite strength to hold his ground? His opponents were soon making mischief, and he was in some real danger. There was considerable trouble in 1543 with the prebendaries or canons of Canterbury who had replaced the conventual rule; they freely levelled against the archbishop charges of favouring heretical preachers, and he might easily be trapped by the Six Articles. The King, however, chaffed him, saying: "O, my chaplain, now I know who is the greatest heretic in Kent," and, on the archbishop asking for a commission of enquiry, insisted that Cranmer himself should be its president, though Cranmer protested that the party accused should not be a member of the commission.

THE ROYAL SUPREMACY

A far graver danger arose when the Council obtained the King's reluctant consent to examine Cranmer and send him to the Tower, so that his accusers would be free to speak. Cranmer's secretary and biographer, Ralph Morice, tells that the archbishop told the King he was willing to go to the Tower, provided he was to be fairly tried in the presence of his accusers. To which the King answered: "O, Lord God! what fond symplicity have you, so to permit yourself to be imprisoned. Do not you think that if they have you once in prison, two or three knaves will be soon procured to witness against you." The King then gave him a ring, to show the Council that he took the matter into his own hands. At eight o'clock next morning the archbishop duly went to the Council Chamber, but, although a member of the Council, he was kept waiting for three-quarters of an hour in an ante-room with serving-men and lackeys. When brought into the chamber, he asked that he might be confronted by his accusers, but they insisted on sending him to the Tower to await trial for having "infested the whole realm of heresy." Then the archbishop said that he was driven to appeal from them to the King, and showed them the ring. On their repairing to the King, he told them: "I would you should well understand that I account my Lord of Canterbury as faithful a man as ever was prelate in this realm. By the faith I owe to

God, whoso loveth me will regard him thereafter." Morice compares this with a saying of Cromwell to Cranmer:

> "You were borne in a happy hower I suppose for, do or say what you will, the Kyng will alwaies well take it at your hande. And I must nedes confess that in some thinges I have complaynyd of you unto his majestie, but all in vayne, for he will never give credit againste you, whatsoever is laied to your charge."

For the remaining years of Henry's reign Cranmer was safe, as others who had served the King—Wolsey, More and Cromwell—were never safe.

Chapter Six

The English Bible and English Litany

THERE was much in the trend of events that must have given Cranmer great uneasiness, with the cause of the Reformation going backwards and forwards, and its opponents still in the ascendancy, and the King capriciously veering this way and that. There was, however, one solid gain in Henry's reign to which the archbishop attached the highest importance, and which he, more than any other man in authority, strove to achieve—the access of the English laity to the Bible in their mother tongue. Tyndale's translations, as we have seen, were proscribed. In the second year of his primacy, Cranmer persuaded Convocation to petition the King for an authorised translation of the Bible. Little came of the project for the moment. Stokesley, Bishop of London, refused to translate the book allotted to him, and answered the archbishop's secretary:

> I marvel what my Lord of Canterbury meaneth, that thus abuseth the people in giving

them liberty to read the scriptures, which doeth nothing else but infect them with heresies, I have bestowed never an hour upon my portion nor never will.

In 1537, the so-called Matthew's Bible appeared; it was probably edited by Tyndale's disciple, John Rogers, who was to be burnt at Smithfield in Mary's reign. It consisted of Tyndale's New Testament, and as much of his Old Testament as he had translated, with the other books (including the Apocrypha) translated by Miles Coverdale. On 4th August, Cranmer sent a copy to Cromwell with a covering letter which included these words:

> I pray you, my Lord, that you will exhibit the book unto the King's highness; and to obtain of his Grace, if you can, a licence that the same may be sold and read of every person, without danger of any act, proclamation, or ordinance heretofore granted to the contrary, until such time that we, the Bishops shall set forth a better translation, which I think will not be till a day after domesday.

Nine days later, Cranmer wrote to thank Cromwell for having procured the King's permission for the book to be bought and read. "You may reckon me your bondman for the same," he writes, "and I dare be bold to say so may you do my Lord of Worcester." Latimer was apparently the first to take advantage of the permission, and to order the prior of Worcester to provide a copy of the Bible to be displayed in the church and the cloister. As a fact, Matthew's Bible had but a short life; just exception was taken to its controversial marginal notes and the very Lutheran prologue to the Epistle to the Romans. Licence for its use was therefore recalled, and revision was entrusted to Miles Coverdale. In this revised form the Great Bible, as it was called from the size of its page, designed for use at the lectern, was ready for distribution before the end of 1539, many difficulties having delayed its printing in Paris and London. The Royal Injunctions of 30th December, 1538, had, therefore, been premature in ordering the clergy to set up the Bible in their churches. The really effective order was in the King's proclamation of 6th May, 1541, that the previous Injunction wherever hitherto neglected, shall now be obeyed; a Bible "of the largest and greatest volume" shall be set up in every parish church for general reading provided that it be not read aloud to the disturbance of divine service and that no layman make "any common disputation" of what he reads. The edition of April, 1540, like the next five editions, included a prologue by the archbishop and is therefore commonly known as Cranmer's Bible. In this preface he makes allowance for those who mistrust what has not been customary, likening them to early man preferring the accustomed diet of "mast and acorns" to the "bread made of good corn" when tillage began to be used. He tells how St. John Chrysostom advised his lay hearers to read the Bible at home, and himself urges how useful it should be to "all manner of persons, of what estate or condition soever they be," whether they are young or old, rich or poor, "lawyers, merchants, artificers, husbandmen." At the same time he warns against irreverent and contentious approach to this "holy Book," " the most precious jewel, and most holy relic that remaineth upon earth." The bishops were, however, far from satisfied with the Great Bible. When it was discussed in Convocation after its publication, they refused to vote that it should be retained "until first duly purged and examined side by side with the (Latin) Bible commonly read in the English Church;" and Gardiner especially wanted the inclusion of many learned words of Latin origin from the Vulgate, such as "imposition of hands" (instead of "laying on") and "Pasch" (for Passover). Committees were appointed to do the revision, but the King let it be known that he wished the work to be entrusted instead to the universities, and nothing more came of the project. It is ominous that no further editions of the Great Bible were printed, after the seventh

ENGLISH BIBLE AND ENGLISH LITANY

edition of December, 1541, until Edward VI's reign. Parliament, in 1543, forbade reading of the Bible, even at home, by women and ignorant people. But Coverdale's Psalms from the Great Bible have been in the liturgical text for just 400 years.

If Cranmer's greatest contribution to the English Reformation was his continuous care for the introduction of the Bible to the people, his next most important service was the provision of a service book in English. Only small beginnings of an English use were possible in Henry VIII's reign. Convocation on 21st February, 1542, ordered that in every parish church a chapter of the New Testament should be read in English, without exposition, after *Te Deum* and *Magnificat*.

In June, 1544, when England was already at war with Scotland, and the King was preparing to invade France with Charles V, the archbishop received a letter from the King (but probably written by Cranmer with the King's assent) directing the use in all parish churches of a "procession" or litany in view of "the miserable state of all Christendom," "so plagued with most cruel wars."

> Forasmuch as heretofore the people, partly for lack of good instruction and calling, partly for that they understood no part of such prayers

or suffrages, as were used to be sung and said, have used to come very slackly to the procession, when the same have been commanded heretofore: we have set forth certain godly prayers and suffrages in our native English tongue.

It was "to be sung or said, as the number of the quire shall serve." This is the origin of the English Litany, the happiest example of the use of English in public worship. It was to be adopted, almost without change in every succeeding edition of the Book of Common Prayer. It is undoubtedly Cranmer's own composition; he drew upon the Sarum Processional, the Roman Breviary, a Latin litany of Luther's, and a collect from the Latin version of the Liturgy of St. Chrysostom, together with some additions of his own.

Cranmer's Litany has been familiar for over four centuries, and its rhythms and cadences have delighted the ear:

> From lightening and tempest, from plage, pestilence and famine, from battaile and murther, and from sodaine death. Good Lorde deliuer us.

> That it may please thee to geue to all nacions unitie, peace, and concorde. We beseche thee to heare us good lorde.

> That it may please thee to succoure, helpe and coumforte all that be in daunger, necessitie and tribulacion: We beseche thee to heare us good lorde.

ENGLISH BIBLE AND ENGLISH LITANY

The reverberation of the word *all* is a token of the catholicity of spirit which moved Cranmer to bring to remembrance all human needs and sorrows in all lands; the litany is an education in charity. There is only one petition which mars this comprehensiveness, and it was happily discarded after 1552: "from the tyranny of the Bishop of Rome and all his detestable enormities." The antiphon or anthem from the Sarum Processional is perfectly Englished:

> O God we have hearde with our eares, and our fathers have declared unto us, the noble workes that thou diddest in theyr dayes, and in the old tyme before them. O Lorde, aryse, helpe us, and deliuer us, for thy honour.

And there is a link with the Christians of the Orthodox Church in the prayer which Cranmer took from the Latin version of the Liturgy called after St. Chrysostom.

Later in this same year he submitted to the King verse translations of several more "processions" for festive days (including some of the great hymns like *Salve festa dies*), suggesting that they might be set to "some devout and solemn note"; "not be full of notes, but, as near as may be, for every syllable a note."

> But by cause mine English verses lack the grace and facility that I would wish they had, your majesty may cause some other to make

95

them again, that can do the same in more pleasant English and phrase.

His diffidence was justified, if we may judge from the example of his verse (if indeed it is his) that has survived in the longer translation of the *Veni Creator* in the Ordinal. Though a master of prose, Cranmer had no gift for writing verse, and he was wise enough to recognize his limitations and suppress these efforts.

The long reign drew to its close, marred near the end by the burning of Anne Askew and three others for heretical views on the Sacrament. The archbishop was not concerned in her trial; Bonner and Gardiner sought to persuade her to recant. The fortitude of this young woman of five-and-twenty no doubt helped to foster the Protestant reaction in the next reign. Six months later, at little past the fifty-fifth anniversary of his birth, Henry died, Cranmer ministering to him after he had become speechless. His will, signed a month before his death, is a lengthy and important document. He begins by repenting his "old and detestable life," desiring the prayers of the Blessed Virgin and furnishing the means for many masses to be said for his soul. By the singular right granted to him by Parliament, it was for him to bequeath the Crown, as he now did to his son Edward, and if Edward should die childless to Mary, and if Mary died without issue, then to

Elizabeth. So in the end, in spite of the Acts depriving them of legitimacy, his three children by Jane Seymour, Catherine of Aragon, and Anne Boleyn were to sit on the throne; and, the Tudors being what they were, their successive reigns would push the cause of the Reformation violently forwards, and violently backwards, then finally establish it. Henry names as "Executors and Counsellors of the Privy Council" during Edward's minority, Cranmer and Tunstall (but not Gardiner), the Earl of Hertford (soon to be Duke of Somerset), twelve other noblemen, knights and judges, and the lay-minded clerical lawyer, Dr. Nicholas Wotton; these men, he declares, "we do make and constitute our Privy Council with our said Son" until he shall have completed his eighteenth year.

What then, were the auguries for the Reformation at Henry's death? It is significant that Gardiner, the upholder of orthodoxy, was omitted from the Council, while Cranmer and Tunstall might be held to balance one another. The laymen were mostly men, prominent in the time of Henry VIII, who had shown a more or less friendly disposition to religious change. Was it possible that Henry's position of Catholicism without the Papacy would endure, or would the logic of events carry the Reformation further than Henry had intended that it should?

Chapter Seven

During Somerset's Protectorate

THE new King's uncle, Edward Seymour, Earl of Hertford, was named only fifth among the councillors for the minority in Henry's will, which remained in Hertford's keeping. A son of one who had been hated for his part in suppressing the Cornish rebels of 1497, he had been enriched and ennobled by Henry VIII and had risen rapidly. In the struggle for control of the regency he had rivals, but some of them were put out of the way in the last weeks of Henry's reign. Norfolk and his son, Surrey, the poet, were suddenly arrested on treasonable charges; the unfortunate Surrey was beheaded a week before the King's death, while his father only escaped death because the act of attainder had not yet been signed when Henry died; he was, however, to remain a prisoner in the Tower for the whole of Edward's reign. Henry's will had contained no suggestion that Hertford should have the leadership; but within a few hours of the proclamation of Edward, the Council, on the motion of Sir William Paget, the late king's chief secretary,

DURING SOMERSET'S PROTECTORATE

chose Hertford as Protector. A few weeks later Hertford became Duke of Somerset and obtained a patent authorizing him to act with or without the assent of Council. Thus for the next three years he enjoyed almost regal power until Parliament deposed him on 14th January, 1550. His rival, John Dudley, now made Earl of Warwick and later to be Duke of Northumberland, for a while acquiesced in Somerset's predominance, though in the end he would overthrow and succeed him. Wriothesley, who had had a notorious part in the examination of Anne Askew by torture, was quickly removed from the Chancellorship and the Council; and Gardiner had not been included by Henry in Edward's Council. Thus the conservative party were without their leading laymen and their most determined cleric, either in Council or in the House of Lords, and the Reformation could go forward without serious opposition. Cranmer's opportunity had at last come.

Yet Protector and archbishop proceeded cautiously. Indeed, Somerset had an attractive quality of moderation, and would fain have produced a religious settlement which would have won the approval, or at least the acquiescence, of the majority of the nation. For the first nine months the Latin mass according to the Sarum use was alone legal, and the Injunctions issued in July allowed no variations, except that Epistle and Gospel were to be read in English, and the Litany to be sung or said in English immediately before mass. Such images "and shrines" as had been "abused with superstition" were to be destroyed; a few months later, on 21st February, 1548, Council abandoned the pretended distinction and ordered the destruction of all images in churches. It can well be imagined how some of the bishops jibbed at being required to see the order carried out and what popular feeling it awoke—either helpless resistance or joining riotously and often illegally in acts of iconoclasm. A book of Homilies was issued at the same time. When a Visitation began in September, Bonner and Gardiner were committed to the Fleet prison for refusing unconditional acceptance of the Injunctions and Homilies, and remained there till the general pardon in the following January; even then they were suspect, and on further charges of recalcitrance they were some months later imprisoned for the rest of the reign. When Parliament met in November, 1547, it repealed the Six Articles and the heresy laws and drastically amended the Treason Act—all the most tyrannous acts of the last reign. Its first Act "against such as shall unreverently speak against the Sacrament of the altar and for the receiving thereof under both kinds" sought to protect "that most high mystery" from the profane abuse of it in speech or press. Convocation had in the same month approved of Communion being given to the laity in both kinds, expressly "not condemning hereby the usage of any Church out of the King's majesty's dominions," and Parliament sanctioned this "except necessity otherwise require," as being "more comfortable to the common use and practice both of the Apostles and of the primitive church." To give effect to this provision *The Order of the Communion* was put out, to come into effect from Easter Day, 1548. The Latin mass was to be said "without the varying of any other rite or ceremony (until other order shall be provided)", except that the new Order should supplement it at the point when the celebrant had received the sacrament. An invitation to communion, a general confession and absolution, the "comfortable words" of Scripture, and a prayer of humble access preceded the administration, all in English. An exhortation, to be used on the Sunday preceding, urged the duty of intending communicants to prepare themselves either by secret confession to the priest or by the use of the general confession now provided, it being left to the conscience of the individual which method he should use. It is reported, on rather doubtful authority, that in one of his last talks Henry VIII had instructed the archbishop to compose a form for the alteration of the mass into a communion. The form was largely modelled on that drawn up by Hermann von Wied, the deposed Archbishop of Cologne. It was at any rate the evident intention of Cranmer, in preparing the new Order, that the aspect of receiving the communion should have precedence over assistance at the mass said by the priest without any communicating but himself.

The greedy spirit of the age was shown in the Act dissolving the Chantries, implementing a similar Act of Henry's reign. The bill was opposed in Parliament by Cranmer, chiefly on the ground that such changes should wait until the King came of age; also he held that better use should be made of the properties now to be sequestrated to the Crown. It is true that a clause provided that such part of the property of a chantry as had been used for the maintenance of a school should continue to be so used, but a great opportunity was missed of diverting far more of the chantry resources to educational purposes. Mr. A. F. Leach and other recent historians have shown that Edward VI has received more credit than is due to him as a founder of grammar schools; the thirty or so that emerged from his reign were of old foundation and were now rather meanly endowed. Christ's Hospital, which was a conversion of the Grey Friars at Newgate, was the best example of a wiser liberality. Latimer, who resumed preaching in Edward's reign after eight years' silence, constantly harped on the need for better educational provision.

> To consider what hath been plucked from abbeys, colleges and chantries, it is marvel no more to be bestowed upon this holy office of salvation.

> If ye will not maintain schools and universities, ye shall have a brutality.

In a sermon preached before King Edward from a pulpit set up in the King's garden because the chapel would not hold all who desired to hear him, he declaimed against this neglect as well as against other social evils of the time:

> For if ye bring it to pass that the yeomanry be not able to put their sons to school (as indeed universities do wondrously decay already) and that they be not able to marry their daughters to the avoiding of whoredom; I say, ye pluck salvation from the people, and utterly destroy the realm.

The time at last seemed propitious for a further advance in religious reform. The destruction of images and shrines, the spoliation of the churches, and the abandonment of many ceremonies thought to be superfluous or even superstitious had gone dangerously far and had excited either lawless image-breaking or sullen resistance. Something more constructive was needed to preserve and stabilize the public worship in order and decency. For many years past, Cranmer had given himself to liturgical study, so far as the materials were available—it was before the days of more scientific and complete liturgiology; the contents of his library show that he had at his service Cardinal Quignon's drastic reshaping of the Breviary, as well as many Lutheran church orders, including Archbishop Hermann's *Consultatio Pia*, which owed much to Bucer, and, as we have seen, he even had access to a Latin version of the Greek Liturgy ascribed to St. John Chrysostom. With a deep sense of reverence, a concern for seemliness and a delicate ear for the harmonies of the English language, he had long been experimenting in the framing of an English service-book. It would be a greater service to the cause of religion than Injunctions and Articles of Faith; *lex orandi*, the regulation of public worship together with a wide circulation of the Bible, would do more to affect the character of the religion of English people for ages to come than definitions of doctrine reflecting the controversies of the time. And here Cranmer was at his best and rendered his greatest service to the Church of England.

A group of bishops and divines, with Cranmer as their chairman and leading spirit, was engaged

DURING SOMERSET'S PROTECTORATE

for many months of 1548, at Windsor and Chertsey, in preparing a Book of Common Prayer. They represented those who favoured old and new opinions, but were agreed in thinking that the church services should be in the mother tongue. Without apparently being submitted to Convocation, the Book was discussed in Parliament and authorized in the first Act of Uniformity. There was considerable discussion in the House of Lords, where the supporters of the Prayer Book among the bishops were only in a very small majority (13 for and 10 against) over those bishops who resisted further change. The stress upon uniformity was perhaps inevitable in the supposed interest of national unity, but it would also be an unfortunate legacy to the future, seeing that men's minds would continue to differ. This first Act of Uniformity (21st January, 1549) did not, however, bear so hardly on the laity as the second (1552); while the clergy were obliged to conform under penalty, there were no penalties on laymen who absented themselves from their parish church, though it was punishable to traduce the Book or interrupt its performance.

There was little criticism of the forms for Matins and Evensong "commonly called Divine Service" now prescribed, and the English Litany had now been in general use for five years. The preface, which was to find a place in every subsequent revision of the Prayer Book, closely and at times verbally follows the preface of Cardinal Quignon to his revised breviary, which was sanctioned by Pope Paul III but, when the Council of Trent revised the breviary, disallowed by Pius V in 1568. Quignon aimed at simplifying the offices by omitting or reducing the number of responds, antiphons, and readings from the lives of the saints, and providing for more continuous readings from the Bible and the whole book of Psalms; he also omitted the offices of the Blessed Virgin. Cranmer's preface, for it is presumably his, deals almost entirely with Mattins and Evensong, those parts of the Prayer Book which attracted least criticism, for there was nothing against Catholic principle in adopting these ancient offices, originally monastic, or in increasing the reading from the Bible and the Psalter. A far more delicate matter was to deal with the mass, but even here much moderation was used, and the result was something of a compromise. Gardiner held that its language would allow of Catholic interpretation, even if the rite was shorn of some of its customary ceremonial.

Although the doctrinal balance of the Prayer Book was considerably altered at its revision in 1552, especially in the Communion Office, the literary standard was maintained; its rhythms and cadences have been a notable English heritage

DURING SOMERSET'S PROTECTORATE

with an even longer history of continued use than the Authorized Version. This is a debt that we owe primarily to Cranmer himself, since, as far as we know, there was no collaborator among his fellow bishops or his chaplains who had anything like the same experience in translating and adapting and composing liturgical texts as the archbishop, who had been assiduously working at them for many years before 1549. It is true that the age was favourable to the composition of beautiful English, as is illustrated in the contemporary work of Thomas More and Miles Coverdale. Cranmer's gift for rendering the ancient collects from the missal and breviary seldom failed him; the harmony and restraint, so congenial in Latin, and so difficult to reproduce in a language which is largely monosyllabic, are generally retained in the English translation, although its brevity and austerity provoked a later Puritan complaint: "The Church casteth forth her ice like morsels; who is able to abide her frost?"

Space will allow only a few examples of translation and of original composition. Here is the version of the fourth century Gelasian Sacramentary:

> Graunte wee beseche thee, mercyfull Lorde, to thy faythfull people, pardon and peace: that they may be clensed from all their sinnes, and serve thee with a quyet mynde: Through Jesus Christ our Lorde.

And this sentence adapted for the Burial Office from Compline for the third Sunday in Lent in the Sarum Breviary:

> Thou knoweste, Lorde, the secretes of our heartes, shutte not up thy merciful eyes to oure prayers: But spare us Lorde moste holy, O God moste mightye, O holy and mercifull saviour, thou most woorthie judge eternall, suffre us not at our last houre for any paynes of death, to fall from thee.

And here are two examples of original composition, a little fuller than the Latin examples:

> Almightie God, whiche haste knitte together thy electe in one Communion and felowship in the misticall body of thy sonne Christe our Lorde: Graunt us grace so to folow thy Saynctes in all vertues, and godly lyvyng, that we maye come to those unspeakeable joyes, whiche thou hast prepared for all them that unfaynedly love thee: through Jesus Christe.

> Almightie God, geve us grace, that we maye caste away the workes of darknes, and put upon us the armour of light, now in the time of this mortal lyfe (in the which thy sonne Jesus Christe came to visite us in great humilitie) that in the last daye, when he shall come again in his gloryous maiestie, to judge both the quicke and the dead: we maye ryse to the lyfe immortall, through him, who liveth and reigneth with thee and the holy gost, nowe and ever. Amen.

DURING SOMERSET'S PROTECTORATE

In the Book of Common Prayer, as A. F. Pollard writes, Cranmer gave to the Church of England "the most effective of all its possessions."

Something remains to be said about the provision of music for the reformed services. Cranmer had already shown an interest in the matter. The English Litany had been sung from its first use in 1544, and in the same year he had tried his hand in translating some of the great festival hymns, hoping that his or some other versions might be matched with appropriate music. They should be sung distinctly and devoutly, like *Te Deum* and *Magnificat*, and in the mass *Gloria in excelsis*, creed, preface, *Sanctus* and *Agnus Dei*. Within a year of the appearance of the new Prayer Book there was issued *The Boke of Common Praier noted*, *i.e.*, set to music, an adaptation of plain chant to the new liturgy, by John Merbecke, organist of the royal chapel of St. George's, Windsor. Five years before, Merbecke had narrowly escaped death for alleged heresy, but while three members of St. George's choir were executed, he obtained a royal pardon on the petition of Bishop Gardiner. For cathedral choirs there was no lack of good polyphonic music for services and anthems, though it may be observed that some of the best composers of the day concealed their preference for the old faith. For the parish churches there was less satisfactory provision. England had no such chorales as helped to popularize the Reformation in Germany or even such lyrical versions of the Psalms as Clement Marot devised for France. Thomas Sternhold dedicated his first slender collection of nineteen psalms "in common metre" to the young king, and a few months after his death in 1549 his friend and neighbour John Hopkins, added eighteen more psalms. In Elizabeth's reign this metrical Psalter was completed, but it must be confessed that Fuller's estimate is not far amiss when he says of the versifiers that "their piety was better than their poetry; and they drank more of Jordan than of Helicon." The use of such metrical psalms might perhaps be covered by the permission given in the first Act of Uniformity to use in churches and chapels "any psalm or prayer taken out of the Bible."

It cannot be said that the Prayer Book of 1549 had a good reception. Parish priests might find it sufficiently near to what was familiar that they could use it with much of the old ceremonial; indeed it was sometimes complained by the more ardent reformers that they "counterfeited" the old services by continued use of the gestures of frequent crossings, although the elevation of the Host at the consecration was now prohibited. In several parts of the country there was open opposition. On the morrow of the introduction of the Prayer Book on Whitsunday, at Sampford

Courtenay, in Devonshire, the parishioners obliged the parish priest (perhaps not unwillingly) to say the Latin mass. The movement rapidly developed in Devon and Cornwall and was accompanied by armed insurrections. The Cornish insurgents sent up their demands to the Council; they asked for the revival of the Six Articles, the restoration of the Latin mass to be celebrated without anyone but the priest communicating except at Easter, the abolition of the English Bible, and the setting up again of images. They demanded also that the lord cardinal Pole who "is of the King's blood" should be pardoned, fetched home, and made a member of Council. They did not, however, ask for the restoration of the papal authority in England.

The archbishop, in his answer, took his stand on the duty of obedience to lawful authority. "Is this the fashion of subjects to speak unto their prince, "We will have?" ... and that saying with armour upon your backs and swords in your hands?" As to the Six Articles of Henry VIII, "within a year or little more, the same most noble prince was fain to temper the said laws." And should the laity be content with communicating at Easter only, whereas Church Councils had for many centuries ordained that they should receive communion at least three times in the year? To the godly, frequent communion "is the greatest comfort that in this world can be imagined." If the Cornishmen complain that "certain of us understand no English," Cranmer replies that fewer of them know Latin. Altogether the reply was better calculated to satisfy Cranmer's own mind than to persuade and convince the disaffected.

While the risings in the West arose directly out of religious grievances, in the East they were caused by agrarian discontent, particularly since the enclosures, a long-standing complaint, had now been aggravated by the greed of the new owners of abbey-lands. The most serious insurrection was in Norfolk, headed by Kett, a tanner. So far from resenting the religious changes, the Norfolk insurgents desired them to go further; under what they called "the Oak of Reformation," the new Prayer Book service was used and Matthew Parker, Elizabeth's future archbishop, preached to them. Protector Somerset, in many ways a humane man, sympathized with the agrarian grievances, and was bitterly reproached in the Council by Paget and Warwick for his leniency in dealing with the rebels. Paget would have had them treated as in the Peasants' War in Germany; "in England it is the feet that govern the head; it is not so in Germany." Warwick suppressed the Norfolk rising in a bloody encounter, and hanged three hundred of the survivors, including Kett and his brother.

DURING SOMERSET'S PROTECTORATE

Warwick seized the occasion of Somerset's lack of firmness, as contrasted with his own ruthless suppression of the rebels, to procure his downfall. Somerset got wind of a cabal within the Council forming against him and meeting in Warwick's London house. On 5th October, he issued leaflets asking for armed support of the King and himself; and, with those Councillors who still stood by him, including Cranmer, he took the young King to Windsor. On 7th October he was proclaimed a traitor, on the authority of the Council; on the 8th, three letters, signed by Cranmer, Sir William Paget and Sir Thomas Smith, were sent "from the Lords of the Council at Windsor to the Lords of the Council in London." The second of these letters is generally taken to be Cranmer's composition, and its terms are characteristic of him. It allows that, since the rumour of the plot has led the Protector to assemble his defences at Windsor, the London Councillors may be excused for making military preparations in their turn; yet the plea is made:

> For the tender passion of Jesus Christ, use your wisdom, and temper your determination in such sort, as no blood be shed, nor cruelty used, neither of his grace's part nor of your lordships': for, if it come to that point, both you and we are like to see presently with our eyes that which every vein of all our hearts will bleed to behold.

> Mary, to put himself (Somerset) simply into your hands, having heard as both we and he have, without first knowledge upon what conditions, it is not reasonable.

But Warwick had secured the support of Wriothesley, the Earl of Arundel and other Catholics, who would welcome Somerset's fall, and also of many of the upper classes who hated his social sympathies. Somerset realized that resistance was vain; he yielded to arrest on 12th October, and on 14th October was lodged in the Tower. Cranmer, like others, was intimidated by Warwick and reluctantly gave him his support.

After a few months in the Tower, Somerset was released and later re-admitted to the Council, but there he was overshadowed by his rival Warwick, who was the effectual ruler of England for the rest of Edward's reign. We can recognize Somerset's lenity in his attempts to procure Gardiner's release from the Tower and to allow the Princess Mary to keep her mass. On fresh charges of treason he was again arrested on 16th October, 1551, and executed on the following 22nd January. Cranmer lost a trusted friend, and the Reformation a far more moderate and sincere guide than the unscrupulous Warwick who supplanted him.

Chapter Eight

Northumberland's Rule

SOMERSET had been popular with the lesser people because of his sympathy with them, but he had his enemies in high places; the nobility and gentry thought he had betrayed their class, the Catholic laity that he had betrayed their faith. He was too optimistic in supposing he could carry through the Reformation without serious opposition; he had sought to be conciliatory, so as to win the support of the Catholic-minded as well as of the more convinced Protestants. When the conservative bishops seemed likely to block the way, they had, like Gardiner and Bonner, suffered short confinement, which had been renewed when they still showed recalcitrance, but none of them was deprived until Northumberland's régime.

By contrast with Somerset's comparative tolerance and willingness to compromise, Northumberland's ruthlessness towards any who stood in his way and his precipitate advocacy of extreme Protestantism earned him widespread hatred and mistrust. Even his sincerity was questioned; it suited his own political and self-regarding ends, rather than his principles, to profess an ardour for the reformed faith, and on the scaffold he confessed himself a Catholic. Like Thomas Cromwell, he was a shrewd Macchiavellian statesman who, in spite of his shrewdness, overshot the mark and provoked the reaction that followed in Mary's reign.

The support which the conservatives had given to Warwick's move encouraged them to hope that there would be a return to the religious position at the end of Henry's reign. Bonner and Gardiner rejoiced at Somerset's overthrow, and mass was celebrated in many Oxford college chapels and elsewhere. But Warwick soon disappointed them. Wriothesley, Earl of Southampton, who had played a leading part in support of Warwick, was soon dismissed from the Council and confined to his house. Arundel was confined to his house too, and Southwell quickly found himself in the Tower, on a trumped-up charge. Warwick, who was now created Duke of Northumberland, adopted or affected for his own ends an extreme Protestant policy. Although he did not become Protector, his power was at least as great as Somerset's had been, and he exercised it almost without check. He intimidated Cranmer and the other members of the Council; indeed, the archbishop ceased to attend the Council regularly, and withdrawing to

NORTHUMBERLAND'S RULE

his diocese watched events from a distance. He gave himself to ecclesiastical administration and to the revision of the Prayer Book and the preparation of Articles of Religion. As a scholar, he must have heard with dismay of the looting of libraries at Oxford by Warwick's agents. The university library was emptied and even its shelves sold. Fuller, a Cambridge man, was later to tell the history of the Oxford library in a simple sentence: "founded by Duke Humphry, confounded by Edward VI's commissioners, refounded by Sir Thomas Bodley." The spoliation of the churches, too, went forward, only the barest necessities for the simplified services being left. The archbishop incurred Northumberland's reproof for his inactivity in such destructive work.

Now that the properties of the monasteries and chantries were secularized, the revenues of the bishoprics attracted the covetous eyes of Northumberland and his adherents. At almost every fresh appointment the bishops were obliged to surrender some of the episcopal manors or to exchange them for property of less value. In particular, Northumberland aimed at acquiring for himself the rich endowments of the see of Durham, to increase his holdings in that area. To effect this, he was determined to deprive Tunstall of his bishopric and annex the larger part of the revenues to the Crown and thence, by immediate grant of the Crown, to himself. After he had committed Tunstall to the Tower for alleged conspiracy, a bill was introduced into the House of Lords to deprive him of his see. Cranmer resisted the bill, although Tunstall had recently attacked the archbishop's sacramental views; but it passed the Lords, with only Cranmer and a single temporal peer voting against it. The Commons showed further resistance, and Northumberland therefore instead procured a commission of lay persons—Cranmer refusing to serve on it—to examine Tunstall's case with power to deprive him, which they proceeded to do. The bishopric of Durham was temporarily dissolved; Tunstall was restored to it on Mary's accession, but he did not take any part in the persecution of Protestants.

In these years Cranmer was paying increased attention to the opinions of continental reformers, especially about the Prayer Book. His personal knowledge of the Protestants had begun with his embassy to Germany in 1532, and he had had much correspondence with Bucer and others without having met them. Their influence on the first reformed Prayer Book was literary rather than personal, owing to Cranmer's acquaintance with the Lutheran service-books. Bucer did not arrive in England until the Prayer Book was already in print, though not yet circulated; but he and others had considerable personal influence on the revision of the book, which was almost at once taken in hand.

Foreign Protestants had already begun to come to this country. At the end of 1547, Peter Martyr Vermigli, named after the Dominican saint, and another Italian, Bernardino Ochino, formerly a famous Capuchin preacher, came to England at Cranmer's invitation and were entertained by him at Lambeth for some months. Cranmer provided Ochino with a prebend at Canterbury. In the following March, Peter Martyr superseded Dr. Richard Smyth as Regius Professor of Divinity at Oxford, where the reforming element was very scantily represented. He was soon engaged in public disputations on the nature of the sacrament. Another Italian scholar, a Jew, who had been converted to Christianity by Pole, but had later become a disciple of Peter Martyr, became a reader in Hebrew at Cambridge.

Cranmer was still hopeful of reaching a common confession of faith in conference with foreign divines, and he invited several leading men to stay with him. John à Lasco (Laski), a Polish count and former Catholic bishop who had adopted extreme Protestant opinions, was invited to attend a conference in August, 1548, and stayed at Lambeth for some months. Of those whom Cranmer invited, most came except Melancthon, whose absence he specially regretted because of

CRANMER—THE ENGLISH REFORMATION

his conciliatory temper and his efforts to bring Lutheran and Swiss theologians to some agreed statute. The unwillingness of many Lutherans to accept the conditions of the Augsburg Interim of 15th May, 1548, imposed by the Emperor as a temporary settlement until the Council of Trent should reach decisions, and the consequent danger to which they exposed themselves, brought many refugees to this country; if England was called by some an asylum, the Imperial ambassador to this country called it "a nest of all infidelity." When Cranmer heard of Bucer's danger he was the more anxious to bring him here and sent him three invitations. At last, in April, 1549, Bucer and his colleague, Fagius, came from Strasburg and were Cranmer's guests for five months until they were provided with the professorships of Divinity and Hebrew at Cambridge. Fagius died in Bucer's arms in November, 1549, very soon after going to Cambridge, and Bucer lived only till 28th February, 1551, but in that short time he won more support for his views, though hotly challenged, than Peter Martyr had done at Oxford.

Somerset also showed favour to the refugees and before long, with the archbishop's approval, they were allowed disused monastic churches in London for their worship. Laski, on his return to England in 1550, became superintendent of the German, French and Italian congregations in

London. Somerset settled a colony of French and Walloon weavers, with Valerendus Pollanus as their minister, on the monastic lands at Glastonbury, which he had acquired.

It will be noticed that Cranmer's guests and correspondents now included representatives of Swiss as well as German theology, and the more advanced Protestantism of Zurich and Geneva was also strongly advocated by John Hooper, who had spent some years as an exile, chiefly in Zurich, and adopted the views of Bullinger, Zwingli's son-in-law and successor. Hooper roundly condemned the Prayer Book of 1549; an Englishman describes him to Bullinger as "an opponent of Lutherans and Bucerians," and fears that the influence of Bucer and Fagius may pervert the archbishop: "May the Lord preserve our England from both of them!" Hooper himself writes to Bullinger soon after Bucer's arrival that he has become the archbishop's "inseparable companion," while the archbishop "did not vouchsafe a word" on receiving a presentation copy of Bullinger's recent theological work.

Cranmer was specially attracted to Bucer, particularly for his mediatory offices to effect an understanding between Lutheran and "reformed" theologians, and even between Protestants and Roman Catholics. Bucer urged Peter Martyr, without much effect, to use less provocative language in the sacramentarian controversy. He himself refused the extreme Zwinglian view of the sacraments being "bare signs" unless it is true that towards the end of life he was coming over to Peter Martyr's views, too late for him to be influencing the archbishop in the revision of the Prayer Book.

Cranmer was affected by the vigorous criticism of the first Prayer Book that came from English and foreign Protestants. Bucer, on the day after he reached Lambeth, wrote, with Fagius, a joint letter to the Ministers of Strasburg, describing their brotherly reception by the archbishop, "that most benevolent and kind father of the churches." They report that in doctrine and rites the forthcoming Prayer Book "is pretty near what could be wished;" that "the Eucharist is administered according to Christ's ordinance" and in the vernacular, and that "private masses" are abolished. There are, indeed, some concessions made to "respect for antiquity and to the infirmity of the present age," such as vestments and lighted candles, but they understand that these are only to be retained for a time lest the people should be deterred by the extensive innovations and so that they may be gradually won over. Bucer himself, like Cranmer, had more respect for tradition than was usual with

Protestants, and Cranmer invited his opinion about vestments, which came to be a matter of urgency when Hooper refused to wear the episcopal habit on being nominated to the see of Gloucester. Bucer would have proposed the abandonment of vestments, but he was prepared to allow them as "indifferent." After Hooper had endured some months of imprisonment for recalcitrance, he, too, recognized them to be indifferent, and was then consecrated. The archbishop's firmness and Hooper's yielding deserve commendation.

There had been no service prescribed in the Prayer Book of 1549 for ordination. This deficiency was ordered by an Act of Parliament of 31st January, 1550, to be made good, and a commission was appointed for the purpose. It is probable that Cranmer had had this need on his mind for some time, and he may even have asked Bucer, while still in his house, to draw up a rite. At any rate the ordination services printed in 1550 have unmistakeable resemblance to the *De Ordinatione Legitima* of Bucer; most of the questions put to the ordinands, the exhortations with their emphasis on the teaching office of the minister, and some of the prayers have their source in Bucer's rite. On the other hand, the doctrinal standpoint of Bucer is rejected, and there is far more conservatism in the English rite,

CRANMER—THE ENGLISH REFORMATION

especially in the wording of the central ordination and consecration, during the laying on of hands. The giving of the chalice and paten to the priest is retained; Bucer took exception to this, and it was omitted when the Ordinal reappeared in the Prayer Book of 1552. For refusing to subscribe to the new Ordinal of 1550, Heath, Bishop of Worcester, was committed to the Fleet by the Council, and six months later he was deprived. Like Tunstall, he was one of the most reasonable and best loved of the bishops.

A weightier task was the revision of the Prayer Book itself. It is evident that Cranmer was desirous of going further, and perhaps from the beginning had meant the first Prayer Book to be provisional only. At the request of Goodrich, Bishop of Ely, Bucer prepared a lengthy criticism, which he finished two months before his death. Its influence on the revised Prayer Book of 1552 can be measured by the number of his criticisms which were adopted as well as by those which were not followed. The words used to communicate at the administration were new and significant, but it was not Bucer who had made this recommendation. They were:

> Take and eate this, in remembrance that Christe died for the, and fede on him in thy heart by faith, with thankes geuyng.

The former words of administration were:

> The body of our Lord Jesus Christ whiche was geuen for thee, preserue thy bodye and soule unto euerlasting lyfe.

These, which would have satisfied the Catholic-minded as compatible with the full doctrine of the Real Presence, were, however, restored in the Elizabethan revision, where they precede the words substituted in 1552. It was about the sacrament that both in England and on the Continent the greatest controversy centred. To give any satisfactory account of this voluminous controversy in so short a book is impossible. It may be sufficient to say that Cranmer by this time had abandoned the mediæval belief which Gardiner, Tunstall and the more conservative churchmen were determined to uphold even at the sacrifice of their freedom and office; this abandonment they regarded as the archbishop's most serious heresy. In 1537 he had upheld against a Swiss divine "this Catholic faith which we hold respecting the real presence" and refused to approve of the opinion maintained by his correspondent. Cranmer's change of mind—which he himself ten years later attributed to the influence of Bishop Ridley, though no doubt others like Bucer and Peter Martyr had affected him—is chiefly revealed in the long works that he wrote in controversy with Gardiner. He had come to think that the practice, as well as the doctrine, of the Eucharist in the mediæval church was a departure from the primitive intention. Whereas it had originally been, as St. Paul described it, a communion, in which the faithful partook, it had come to be the offering of a sacrifice by the priest, at which the faithful were present without communicating; besides, unless they knew Latin, they could only follow the general outline of the service and bring it home to themselves by their private and individual prayers. Cranmer pleaded that the very words of the mass presumed that the laity communicated; he cited the petition "that so many of us as receive the sacred body and blood of thy Son by this participation of the altar may be fulfilled with grace and benediction"; yet the laity commonly communicated at Easter only or three times in the year. He desired that the faithful should communicate every Lord's Day, as appeared to be the practice described in the Acts of the Apostles. In this expectation he was to be disappointed, as neither in England nor on the Continent did weekly Communion become general, although it became commoner.

Cranmer also thought that the aspect of the Eucharist chiefly emphasized by mediæval practice and theory was that it was a propitiatory sacrifice offered by the priest for the living and the dead. The belief in Purgatory further heightened the importance of this aspect and led to the multiplication of masses for the dead, provided through payments made by the living for their departed kinsfolk and friends or through the wills of the departed themselves. Such masses were oftener than not celebrated by the priest with no one present but a server. These "private masses" were among the "abuses" brought forward by the Lutheran delegates in their conference with the English bishops and divines nominated by Henry VIII in 1538, but the King was stiff in allowing no concession on this head and the Six Articles of the next year enacted that "private masses be continued." Cranmer also feared that the emphasis on the sacrificial aspect of the Eucharist confused the popular mind, leading the uninstructed to suppose that it was a repetition, rather than a remembrance, of Christ's "full, perfect and sufficient sacrifice" upon the Cross. Gardiner himself agreed that in the mass there was no "repetition" of this sacrifice. Cranmer quoted in support of his view, Peter Lombard, the famous mediæval "Master of the Sentences," who said: "That which is offered and consecrated by the priest is called a sacrifice and oblation, because it is a memory and representation of the true sacrifice and oblation made on the altar of the cross." Accordingly, the Prayer Book, from 1549 onwards, dwells upon the Eucharist as a "perpetual memory" of Christ's sacrificial death, and the communicant is bidden to receive the sacrament "in remembrance that Christ died for thee"; the only sacrifice, except that of Calvary, that is explicitly mentioned as belonging to the Eucharist is the offering of "ourselves, our souls and bodies," in "this our Sacrifice of praise and thanksgiving." The Forty-two Articles of Religion, which were being worked out at the time when the Prayer Book of 1552 came into use, maintained the sufficiency of "the perfect (or "unique," 1561), sacrifice of Christ made upon the cross" and condemned "the sacrifice of masses, in which it was commonly said that the priests did offer Christ for the quick and the dead, to have remission of pain or sin."

There was the further distressing controversy about the nature of Christ's presence in the sacrament. This was the very touchstone of orthodoxy for men like Tunstall and Gardiner. There was more chance of conciliation with the Lutheran view—"consubstantiation"—which was a high doctrine, if also at least as difficult as that of transubstantiation and with far less support from tradition, but at this second stage of the English Reformation the Zwinglian and other Swiss doctrines were exercising more influence than the Lutheran. According to his own account

Cranmer did not pass through a Lutheran stage of belief about the sacrament, but, about 1546, went straight from the mediæval to his final view. He did not accept the negative view of the Zwinglians that the sacraments were "bare signs"; they were defined in the Forty-two Articles as "effectual signs of grace," that is, they not only typify but convey to the faithful that which they signify. Cranmer was insistent that Christ was "spiritually" present to the faithful receiver "in the ministration of the sacrament," but unwilling to assert that he was present "really" or "carnally" in the consecrated elements.

The traditional belief was that at consecration the "substance" of the bread and wine was transmuted into the Body and Blood of Christ. Both Gardiner and Tunstall admitted that they could not say how this change was effected. "How Christ is present" Gardiner allowed, "I cannot tell"; and Tunstall similarly said: "how the bread was changed into his body, all the most learned of the ancients deemed inscrutable." They were content to accept literally the words of Christ recorded in the New Testament, and to accept loyally also the definitions of the Church; and they viewed with the gravest concern and alarm Cranmer's rejection of the customary epithets "real" and "corporal."

On the other hand, Cranmer desired the

CRANMER—THE ENGLISH REFORMATION

sacrament to be received with the utmost devotion. When Hooper, John Knox and John à Lasco were contending that this revised Prayer Book of 1552 should abandon the ancient practice of the communicant kneeling to receive the sacrament, he refused to give way. The Council were minded to concede the point, but when they referred it to the archbishop, he wrote this spirited answer:

> Your lordships are wise, but is it wisdom to alter without Parliament what has been concluded by Parliament at the bidding of glorious (i.e. vainglorious) and unquiet spirits, who would still find faults if the Book were altered every year? They say that kneeling is not commanded in Scripture, and what is not commanded in Scripture is unlawful. There is the root of the errors of the sects! If that be true, take away the whole Book of Service; and let us have no more trouble in setting forth an order in religion, or indeed in common policy. If kneeling be not expressly enjoined in Holy Scripture, neither is standing or sitting. Let them lie down on the ground, and eat their meat like Turks or Tartars.

Without reference back to Parliament, the Council ordered the insertion of what is known as the Black Rubric, which defends the rubric that prescribes kneeling, on the ground that it is intended only "to avoid profanation and disorder," but explains:

it is not mente thereby, that any adoration is doone, or oughte to bee doone, either unto the Sacramentall bread or wyne there bodelye receyved, or unto anye reall and essenciall presence there beyng of Christe's naturall fleshe and bloude. For as concernynge the Sacramentall bread and wyne, they remayne styll in theyr verye naturall substances.

When the Prayer Book was again revised at the beginning of Elizabeth's reign, this rubric, being without Parliamentary authority, was omitted; and when it was again inserted in 1661 there was the significant change of "corporal" for "real and essential."

The Prayer Book of 1552 and the Articles of 1559 represent the furthest stage in the Protestant direction that the English Reformation reached, but this Prayer Book was in use for only eight months (from All Saints Day, 1552) and the Articles for a few weeks only before Edward VI's death, and at each subsequent revision of them—of the Prayer Book in 1561, 1609 and 1661, and of the Articles in 1563 and 1571—a more even balance between tradition and change was achieved. In spite of compromises, the formularies of the end of Edward VI's reign probably express Cranmer's final views with some exactness: but they were not final for the Church of England. The debt to Cranmer is very great, especially for his liturgical skill and for his advocacy of an

English Bible at a time when few bishops supported it, but that debt has never meant servility. Whether Cranmer intended it or not, the Prayer Book has admitted more than one interpretation and has left a considerable latitude of opinion to those who have loyally accepted it with more regard for what it says than for Cranmer's personal interpretation or intention. The Articles of Religion, with a more deliberate intention of mediating than of accentuating differences, avoid the inelastic hardness of the contemporary Continental confessions of faith. As a learned Presbyterian writer, Dr. John Tulloch, said of them:

> There is present everywhere a touch of moderation, the softening influence of a conciliatory doctrinism which is true to the positive aspects of Augustinianism and the evangelical import of the great questions raised by the Reformation, but which yet shrinks, for the most part, from all negative and extreme deductions.

The pace and violence of Northumberland's religious policy were clearly distasteful to Cranmer's sober and orderly mind. Cranmer's resistance to the wholesale spoliation of the Church, its revenues and its adornments, brought upon him Northumberland's displeasure. He even told Queen Mary that the Duke had sought "long time my destruction." He was little con-

NORTHUMBERLAND'S RULE

sulted, he was often hotly reproved for inactivity. "For Heaven's sake," wrote Northumberland to Cecil on 28th October, 1552, "make Knox Bishop of Rochester. He will be a whetstone to Cranmer, who needs one." But fortunately Knox declined the bishopric.

Cranmer's most serious difference with Northumberland arose at the very end of Edward's reign over the Succession. By a unique concession of Parliament, Henry VIII had been allowed to name the successors to the throne in the event of Edward's having no issue. In his will he nominated Mary, then Elizabeth if Mary left no issue, and then, if Elizabeth also was childless, the heirs of his sister Mary, Duchess of Suffolk. Northumberland, realizing that Edward was dying in his minority, and believing that his own tenure of power and perhaps even his own life would end with the accession of Mary, gambled on the wild chance of diverting the succession. Six weeks before Edward's death, he married his elder unmarried son, Lord Guilford Dudley, to Lady Jane Grey. Her grandmother, Henry VIII's sister, was long dead, but her mother Frances, married to Henry Grey, now Duke of Suffolk, was still alive but willing to surrender her claim to the throne to Jane.

Chapter Nine

The Marian Reaction

JANE, born in the same month as Edward VI (October, 1537), was not yet sixteen years of age. Precociously learned, pious and dutiful, she was unable to withstand either her parents' disposal of her in marriage to so unsuitable a bridegroom, or Northumberland's ambitious schemes for her. In imitation of Henry's will, but without the Parliamentary sanction that Henry had, Northumberland persuaded the dying King to "devise" the throne to his cousin Jane. Cranmer had seldom been present at meetings of the Council, and at any rate his name does not appear among the signatures on 11th and 14th June, of Councillors who summoned the high legal officers of the Crown and other judges to attend in order to draw up in due form Edward's "devise." Sir Edward Montagu, formerly Lord Chief Justice, later wrote a memorandum of those fateful meetings. He and the other men of law were brought on 12th June into the presence of the King, who told them of his intention to prevent the succession of Mary who "might

THE MARIAN REACTION

marry a stranger-borne, whereby the Laws of this Realm might be altered and changed, and His Highness's proceedings in Religion might be altered." They protested that this "was directly against the Act of Succession, which was an Act of Parliament which would not be taken away by no such devise." When the King still insisted, they asked for reasonable time "to consider the Laws and Statutes made for the Succession." On the morrow they were all agreed that it would be treason, on the part of the Council as well as of themselves, to be implicated in any proceeding for setting aside the existing provision for Edward's successors. On their recall to Council they stated their opinion. Northumberland was not present but, being advised of their answer, he entered the council-chamber "in a great rage and fury, trembling for anger" and declared that "he would fight in his shirt with any man in that quarrel." A second time they were brought into the presence of the King, who received them "with sharp words, and angry countenance." Again they protested that the Acts of Succession "will not be taken away, but by the same authority they were made, and that was by Parliament." Northumberland "ruled the whole Council as it pleased him, and they were all afraid of him (the more is the pity)," and the lawyers agreed to do what was asked of them, on the King's issuing to them a licence under the Great Seal and granting them a pardon signed with his own hand. The "devise" or will (Edward, as a minor, was not of legal age for making a will) was drawn up and signed on 21st June by the members of Council. The young William Cecil, a Secretary of State, signed, but according to his own account only as a witness to the King's signature, and he relinquished the office of secretary to his brother-in-law, Sir John Cheke.

Cranmer was the last of all to sign. As he explained his "heinous folly and offence" later in a letter to Queen Mary, his request "to talk with the King's majesty alone," when he hoped that he might have "altered him from that purpose," was refused, as he was only allowed to see him in the presence of Lord Northampton, Lord Darcy and others. The King and the Council informed him that the judges upheld Edward's right to dispose of the Crown.

> This seemed very strange unto me; but being the sentence of the Judges, and other his learned counsel in the laws of this realm (as both he and his Council informed me) methought it became not me, being unlearned in the law, to stand against my Prince therein. And so at length I was required by the King's Majesty himself to set to my hand to his will; saying, that he trusted that I alone would not be more repugnant to his will, than the rest

of the Council were; (which words surely grieved my heart very sore) and so I granted him to subscribe to his will, and to follow the same. Which when I had set my hand unto, I did it unfeignedly and without dissimulation.

It was a grievous error of Cranmer to give in against his judgment, but it is consistent with his general line of conduct. With his deep sense of duty to the Crown he had always felt bound to yield obedience, sometimes straining his conscience to do so, and, often after prolonged and stiff opposition to a measure while it was still under discussion, as, for instance, the Bill of the Six Articles, in the end subordinating his judgment to that of the King and Parliament when a decision had been reached. His life-long loyalty to King Henry would make him the more unwilling to be a party to the setting aside of Henry's will, to the execution of which he, like other Councillors, had been sworn. In a letter of 23rd April, 1554, he reminds the Lords of the Council that they can testify how he "spake against" Edward's "will"; "I refer me to the reports of your honours;" they can testify, if they are honest, to the fact of his opposition. But in the end he found himself unable to resist the personal appeal of the dying King.

The King's death on 6th July, 1553, was kept secret for two days, and then Jane was proclaimed

Queen. Northumberland failed to secure the person of Mary, who quickly rallied supporters, and indeed, she was at once being acknowledged as the rightful sovereign in many parts of the country. After nine days, Jane's own father, the Duke of Suffolk, proclaimed Mary at Tower Hill, and on the next day, 20th July, even Northumberland, who had headed troops to put down resistance, proclaimed Mary at Cambridge. The Earl of Arundel arrested him and brought him to the Tower. Mary, attended by Elizabeth, entered London on 3rd August, and the national will that she should be queen was evident.

Why did not Cranmer flee abroad, as so many of the Edwardian bishops did? Was it because he was too closely watched, or did he, with his optimistic temperament, still hope that the cause of the Reformation might be saved? It was not then certain that Mary's accession would mean a return to the papal obedience. There was no doubt of her personal allegiance to the old faith, but there was still a possibility that there might be a return to the religious position at the end of Henry's reign or even that some considerable part of the Edwardian reforms would be allowed. An index of the temporary co-existence of new and old is that a mass and dirge were sung for Edward in Mary's presence at the Tower and that the archbishop conducted the

THE MARIAN REACTION

Burial Office and celebrated the Holy Communion in Westminster Abbey according to the rites of the Prayer Book which was still the law of the land. Fifteen days after Mary's arrival in London, her first Proclamation about religion was published (18th August, 1553). The Queen expresses her resolve to maintain openly the religion she had "ever professed from her infancy hitherto" and her desire that "the same were of all her subjects quietly and charitably embraced." She is not minded to compel her subjects "unto such time as further order, by common assent, may be taken therein." Like her father she means to get sanction for any changes in religion. Meanwhile disorder and provocative words—"papist or heretic and such like"—must be avoided; unauthorised preaching and unlicensed printing of controversial matters are forbidden under penalty.

For several months there was the utmost variety of usage. In many parish churches the Prayer Book continued to be used, while in others the mass was celebrated in anticipation of the expected change in the law. The archbishop denied a rumour that after Mary's accession he had celebrated the Latin mass at Canterbury, though his suffragan had done so without his authorization. He also stated his willingness to defend the Prayer Book and condemn the mass, and therefore he was called before the Council on 8th September for disseminating seditious libels, and committed to the Tower. A little while before, he had been summoned to Council for his participation in Queen Jane's affair and put under house arrest in Lambeth, pending further proceedings. In a letter to Cecil he says that he had seen him at court and "would fain have talked" to him, but refrained from doing so, for the sake of Cecil, who was in some danger because of his very limited complicity in the matter of Edward VI's will, the archbishop wished to avoid implicating him further. On 13th November, Cranmer, the Lord Guilford Dudley, the Lady Jane and others were tried for treason, found guilty and sentenced to death. The Queen, however, spared Cranmer's life, and he was attainted by Parliament, which involved his deprivation; he was henceforth described as "the late Archbishop of Canterbury," though his degradation was postponed till 1556.

Latimer also—a broken old man of eighty— was sent to the Tower for "seditious demeanour." Ridley had been imprisoned there on 25th July, Hooper had been committed to the Fleet, and Ferrar was ultimately sent to the Queen's Bench prison.

Four bishops, including Hooper and Ferrar, were deprived for being married men, and at least four fled abroad and remained there till Elizabeth's accession. Three of the bishops deprived in Edward's reign—Gardiner, Heath and Day—were at once reinstated, and, a little later, after their appeals had been heard, Barnes and Tunstall. In 1554, ten bishops were appointed by virtue of Mary being still the Supreme Head; she detested that title, but it was too advantageous to be discarded yet. In a consistory at Rome, in July, the Pope "provided" nine of these bishops, although England was still technically in schism. Foreign Protestants were allowed to leave the country.

When Parliament met in the autumn, with Gardiner, now Lord Chancellor, presiding, it repealed nine Edwardian statutes concerning religion, including the Act of Uniformity of 1552, but the Prayer Book might be used without molestation until 20th December, after which the Latin services must alone be used as in the last year of Henry's reign. Julius III appointed Reginald Pole *legatus a latere* on 5th August, 1553, and correspondence passed between legate and Queen. Mary was obliged to tell Pole that the time was not yet ripe for reconciliation with the Holy See. The emperor and the French king, as well as Mary herself, put obstacles in the way of the legate's premature return, and sixteen months of her reign were to pass before he reached this country.

Even the Acts of Parliament validating Henry's marriage with Catherine and consequently affirming Mary's legitimacy made no mention of the Pope. At the time of Pole's appointment his outlawry was not yet rescinded and he had been so long out of England that he had no adequate knowledge of English opinion; he mistrusted many of Mary's bishops who had earlier committed themselves to the principle of the Royal Supremacy, while, as Mary was forced to recognize, many of the most Catholic laymen had to be assured that they would not be asked to disgorge the monastic spoils which they had acquired. Pole for long resisted the latter condition, but the Pope took a less stringent view and, reluctantly of course, agreed to leave the former church property in lay hands.

At the beginning of 1554, Spanish ambassadors arrived to treat for Mary's marriage to Philip. The projected marriage was intensely unpopular, and Sir Thomas Wyatt put it in the foreground of his rebellion that broke out later in the month. It was speedily suppressed, but it sealed the fate of some who had no concern in it. Lady Jane Grey, her husband, uncle and father, who had been in the Tower since November, were now brought to the block. Cranmer and the other bishops in prison had no connexion with the rebellion, which indeed made almost no mention of religion. Many executions followed but all of them for treason, not ostensibly for religion; there were no burnings for heresy till 1555.

Cranmer, after being in the Tower exactly six months, was taken with Ridley and Latimer to Oxford, and lodged in Bocardo, a little lock-up building near the old North Gate and St. Michael's Church. On Saturday, 14th April, 1554, they were brought before a large body of commissioners, representing the Lower House of Convocation and the universities of Oxford and Cambridge, and told that they would be required to answer questions on the nature of the sacrament in the Divinity School, Cranmer on the following Monday, Ridley on Tuesday, Latimer on Wednesday. When Cranmer, alone and without counsel, faced the thirty-three divines for six hours on end, he bore himself with becoming humility and patience. Dr. Warton, Dean of Westminster, as Prolocutor of the Lower House, announced in his first sentence from the chair that they were met together to denounce damnable heresy about the sacrament, and, as Convocation had already judged Cranmer's views to be heretical, there could be little use in further disputation. Cranmer at once remarked:

> We are assembled to discuss these doubtful controversies, and to lay them open before the eyes of the world; whereof ye think it unlawful

to dispute. It is indeed no reason that we should dispute of that which is determined upon before the truth be tried. But if these questions be not called into controversy, surely mine answer then is looked for in vain.

For nearly six hours the archbishop was bombarded with questions, his mild voice being drowned at times by interruptions, hissing and clapping, and even insulting epithets, from which the chairman did not protect him. As Cranmer reported in a letter to the Lords of the Council at the end of the week:

I never knew nor heard of a more confused disputation in all my life. For albeit there was one appointed to dispute against me, yet every man spake his mind, and brought forth what him liked without order. And such haste was made, that no answer could be suffered to be given fully to any argument, before another broke in with a new argument. And in such weighty and large matters there was no remedy, but the disputations must needs be ended in one day, which can scantly well be ended in three months.

Though he must have known the danger he ran, he argued calmly and ably, and held to his honest opinions. When he was pressed to say whether he agreed with the teaching of the Church that the Body of Christ was "really" present in the Sacrament and "as showed us upon the earth," he replied that if "really" meant "effectually," he agreed, but if it meant "corporally" he must refuse, as in his view "No man seeth Christ upon the earth; he is seen with the eyes of our mind, with faith and spirit." He refused the doctrine of transubstantiation and maintained, as he had consistently done for some years now, that Christ's sacrifice on the Cross was sufficient propitiation for the sins of all mankind, and needed no repetition. Although it was obvious that he could not hope to satisfy his interlocutors and must expect condemnation, he was, strangely enough, allowed to take part on the Thursday in the customary academic disputation to which John Harpsfield must submit before his admission to the degree of Doctor of Divinity. At the end the president expressed himself:

> Your wonderful gentle behaviour and modesty, good Mr. Doctor Cranmer, is worthy much commendation: and that I may not deprive you of your right and just deserving, I give you most hearty thanks in mine own name, and in the name of all my brethren.

And at these words, "all the doctors quietly put off their caps." Nevertheless, on the next day the commissioners condemned the opinions of the three bishops, and they were taken back to Bocardo, though their fate was still undetermined.

Gardiner had begun by opposing the marriage project, but he became reconciled to it, drew up as favourable terms as could be devised to protect English interests, and himself celebrated the wedding in his own cathedral church on 25th July, the feast of St. James, patron saint of Spain. The King and Queen now had identical styles, being associated as joint sovereigns, but Mary herself resisted Philip's desire to be crowned. Now that the marriage was achieved, the way was clear for reconciliation with Rome. In the new Parliament that met on 12th November, 1554, Gardiner, the Lord Chancellor, in his opening speech, announced that they were summoned "for the confirmation of true religion." Pole's attainder was at once rescinded and a Supplication was addressed by both Houses to the King and Queen for the reception of the realm "into the bosom and unity of Christ's Church." On 30th November Parliament received on their knees the legate's absolution, and on 6th December the members of Convocation were pardoned "for all their perjuries, schisms and heresies." Parliament proceeded to repeal the religious statutes passed in Henry's reign from the beginning of the Reform Parliament of 1529, now that "the lord Cardinal Pole, legate *de latere*" had come "to call us home again into the right way from whence we have all this long while wandered and stayed abroad." The Queen and the legate had been obliged to pay a price for this submission; the same Act was careful to set out in full that those who had been granted church property were confirmed in their possessions and might enjoy them "without scruple of conscience" or danger from church censure.

A rigorous policy for the extirpation of heresy was at once adopted. The heresy laws of Henry IV and V were revived, to take effect from the following 20th January. Within a few days of the Act becoming operative, John Rogers, the maker of Matthew's Bible, was burnt at Smithfield, Rowland Taylor was sent to be burnt in his own parish of Hadleigh in Suffolk, and Bishop Hooper in his own city of Gloucester, just as Bishop Ferrar a few weeks later was burnt in his own diocese of St. David's. Gardiner, who had accepted and defended all of Henry VIII's religious changes hoped that a few such examples would be sufficiently deterrent, and there were no burnings in his diocese. He died on 12th November, 1555, nine months after the persecution had begun. In the northern dioceses, too, there was only a single execution, Tunstall of Durham especially being averse from such methods of upholding the faith. Bonner, however, showed no such unwillingness, and London had long been a gathering place of those favourable to the Reformation. In the remaining two years and nine months of Mary's reign nearly three hundred, including obscure lay-folk and women, were burnt. The fate of the three bishops imprisoned at Oxford was still undetermined. Latimer and Ridley were brought to trial by three bishops commissioned by Pole as legate, condemned, and burnt "in the ditch over against Balliol College," on 16th October, 1555.

Chapter Ten

Cranmer's Trial and Execution

THE case of Cranmer, as archbishop, was reserved for papal direction, at the request of the King and Queen. Already, a few months before his fellow-bishops were tried, he was served with a writ citing him to appear at Rome within eighty days, personally or by proxy, to answer charges brought against him by the King and Queen. He wrote to the Queen about the citation to Rome:

> If your majesty will give me leave, I will appear there. And I trust that God shall put in my mouth to defend his truth there as well as here.

It was perhaps never intended that Cranmer should appear at Rome, and instead his trial was delegated by the prefect of the Inquisition, on Pope Paul IV's instructions, to James Brooks, Master of Balliol, who had succeeded Hooper as Bishop of Gloucester the year before, and four other commissioners; they were to report their findings to Rome, where sentence would be pronounced. The previous trial of April, 1554, held before the restoration of papal authority in England, was regarded as void.

On 12th September, 1555, Cranmer's trial was begun in the university church of St. Mary the Virgin, at Oxford. Bishop Brooks, representing the Pope, sat on a scaffold ten feet high in front of the high altar, and below him were the two "proctors" (or prosecutors) of the King and Queen, Martin and Story, doctors of the civil law. Cranmer was charged with blasphemy, incontinency (*i.e.*, for his marriage), and heresy. He began by confessing his inability in conscience to acknowledge the jurisdiction of the Pope, a foreigner. Brooks opened the proceedings; addressing Cranmer as "my lord," he was courteous and kindly. Who, he asked, had been thought "more devout" and more earnest in defence of the sacrament of the altar than Cranmer had once been? He would speak, he said, "to your comfort": "We come not to judge you, but to put you in remembrance of that you have been, and shall be ... if you be moved to come to a conformity." Perhaps the bishop went beyond what the Queen would have implemented when he said to Cranmer:

> When you were Archbishop of Canterbury and Metropolitan of England, it is ten to one (I say) that you shall be as well still, yea and rather better. For as Saint Paul after his conversion was received into the Church of Christ, with wonderful joy to the whole congregation,

CRANMER'S TRIAL AND EXECUTION

even so shall you be. The fame of your return shall be spread abroad throughout all Christendom, where your face was never known.

If Cranmer had seen abuses in the Church, was that sufficient reason for forsaking the Church of Christ? "You should rather have endeavoured for a reformation than for a defection." Let him not think himself wiser than all Christendom, but humbly return to the unity of the Catholic Church.

Very different from the bishop's were the opening speeches of the two proctors. "Thomas Cranmer" is termed "this stubborn heretic," who gains nothing by his vainglorious babble, and has "no conscience." It must be admitted that there were weak points in Cranmer's armour which Dr. Martin did not fail to pierce. How came he to condemn John Lambert for sacramentarian opinions which he now held himself? And if the prince is supreme head of the Church in his own realm, "what say you by Nero?" Cranmer, thus posed, answered that Nero was head "in worldly respect of the temporal bodies of men," of whom the Church consisted. Cranmer stoutly maintained that though Christ alone was supreme head of the Church and had appointed no vicar, yet the King of England "holdeth his crown and sceptre of himself, by the ancient laws, customs and descents of the kings of this realm," and he rejected the Pope's claim "that all emperors and kings hold their crowns and regalities of him, and that he may depose them when he list; which is high treason for any man to affirm and think, being born within the King's dominions."

There was still some hope that Cranmer might be reconciled to Rome. He had always a sincere respect for the authority of the Crown. As he had written to Queen Mary: "I will never, God willing, be author of sedition, to move subjects from the obedience of their heads and rulers." Now that Parliament and Convocation, as well as the King and Queen, had accepted papal authority, he might be willing to defer to this as having the fullest legality. His earlier undated submissions go so far and no further. With his sensitive and academic mind, that sought agreement and saw both sides of a question, he might yet be brought to some accommodation. Nor was so sensitive a man free from the fear of the cruel death that had befallen his fellow prisoners. It would have been a greater triumph to secure the submission of the former protagonist of the English Reformation and pension him off in obscurity than to antagonize a considerable part of the English people by bringing him, like the other four bishops, to the stake. At one stage—the date is not known—he was removed from prison to the deanery at Christ Church, where he was treated civilly, took exercise in the bowling

CRANMER'S TRIAL AND EXECUTION

green, and was plied with persuasive arguments by a Spanish friar.

It was a foregone conclusion that Bishop Brooks should report to Rome that Cranmer was convicted of heresy. The consistory at Rome on 4th December, after the eighty days had elapsed since the citation without his appearing in person or by proxy, deprived him and sentenced him to be delivered to the secular arm. The papal order for his degradation followed, and on 14th February, 1556, the humiliating ceremony was performed in the cathedral church at Oxford. Thomas Cranmer was dressed up in the vestments of priest and bishop and the archbishop's pallium, all of coarse canvas, and a crozier put into his hand. Then began the humiliating process of stripping him of these symbols of office. When they took the crozier from him he made some resistance and took from his sleeve a written appeal from the Pope to the next General Council, and protested that, the matter at issue being between the Pope and himself *immediate*, "no man ought to be a judge in his own cause." When they took the pallium from him, he said, "Which of you hath a pall, to take off my pall?" meaning that they were his ecclesiastical inferiors. Lastly, Bishop Bonner scraped the top of the archbishop's fingers where they had been anointed. It was noted that while Bonner, the presiding bishop, showed some roughness, his assessor, Bishop Thirlby, was in tears, calling it "the most sorrowful action of his whole life," for Cranmer had always a deep affection for him "and thought nothing too much to give him or to do for him." Cranmer was then dressed in a poor yeoman's garment with a townsman's cap.

In the five weeks that remained before his being taken to the stake he was still pressed to recant. It was not enough that he should already have acknowledged the Pope's supremacy in accordance with the laws of the land and have submitted his book on the sacrament "to the judgment of the Catholic Church, and of the next General Council." Two days after his degradation he subscribed a statement that he accepted unfeignedly the teaching of the Catholic Church on the sacraments and all articles of the faith. There followed a precise submission and complete recantation in which he anathematized the teachings of Luther and Zwingli and explicitly accepted the doctrines of transubstantiation and purgatory. This document was attested by Friar John de Villa Garcia and Henry Sidall, a former disciple of Peter Martyr, who accepted the changes under Mary and Elizabeth with equal celerity. This real recantation of all his convictions was at once published; it was well calculated to discredit him in the eyes of those who had shared his convictions. Perhaps it

CRANMER'S TRIAL AND EXECUTION

was the same spiritual advisers who drew up for him to sign on 13th March the most abject submission in which he confessed himself to have been the cause of the schisms and heresies that had afflicted his country and likened himself to the penitent thief on the Cross. On the morning of his execution the friar induced him to sign his seventh submission, which he was meant to read aloud in the last scene of his life.

On 21st March, 1556, the day before Passion Sunday, Cranmer, with two friars walking beside him, was brought by the mayor to St. Mary's Church, where a stage had been erected for him opposite the pulpit; the incision into the pillar for the fastening of the stage is still visible. Confronted with the great congregation, this shy man turned his face to the pillar and secretly prayed until the preacher, Henry Cole, Provost of Eton, mounted the pulpit. With tears running down his face, "the very image and shape of perfect sorrow," Cranmer listened while Cole justified his execution in spite of his recent confession of the Catholic faith, on the ground that Bishop Fisher's death, already avenged by the burning of four bishops, required yet another to make the balance equal. Yet, as Cranmer had at last come home to the true faith, the preacher bid him take this comfort, that there should be masses for his soul in all the churches of Oxford. He then bade all make silent prayer for Cranmer, and a spectator who adhered to the old faith remarked:

> I think there was never before such a number so earnestly praying together. For they that hated him before, now loved him for his conversion, and hope of continuance. They that loved him before could not suddenly hate him, having hope of his confession again of his fall. So love and hope increased devotion on every side.

Cole then called upon Cranmer to proclaim his recovered faith. Cranmer began by humbly entreating God's forgiveness for all his sins, and at the point when he said, "There is one offence which most of all at this time doth vex and trouble me," there was the general expectation that he would read his latest recantation. Instead he drew from his bosom a beautiful prayer of his own composition which he then read, and a written exhortation. The latter was free from all controversial matter; he bid the people "obey your King and Queen, willingly and gladly," exhorted them to charity and "to hurt no man, no more than you would hurt your own natural loving brother or sister." It is characteristic of him that even in this hour of his own destruction he should commend the cause of the humble to the generosity of the more fortunate, "for if they ever had occasion to show their charity, they have it now at this present, the poor people being so many,

CRANMER'S TRIAL AND EXECUTION

and victuals so dear." After reciting the Apostles' Creed, he used these words, introducing them with a sentence which must have led his hearers to expect from him his latest recantation which would be so great a triumph for his opponents:

> And now I come to the great thing, that so much troubleth my conscience, more than any thing that ever I did or said in my whole life; and this is the setting abroad of a writing contrary to the Truth; which now here I renounce and refuse, as things written with my hand, contrary to the truth which I thought in my heart, and written for fear of death, and to save my life, if it might be; and that is, all such bills and papers which I have written or signed with my own hand since my degradation; wherein I have written many things untrue. And forasmuch as my hand offended, writing contrary to my heart, my hand shall first be punished therefore; for, may I come to the fire, it shall be first burned.

In two sentences that followed he abjured the Pope and stood by his former book on the sacrament. There was an immediate outcry at this unexpected recantation of his recantations, and he was pulled down from the stage and hustled along the street to the ditch opposite Balliol College, where Latimer and Ridley had been burned.

After kneeling in prayer he stripped himself of his shirt, bared his head and feet, shook hands

CRANMER—THE ENGLISH REFORMATION

with some of the bystanders (a young Fellow of Brasenose College refusing his hand), and so went to the stake.

> And when the wood was kindled, and the fire began to burn near him, stretching out his arm, he put his right hand into the flame, which he held so steadfast and immovable (saving that once with the same hand he wiped his face) that all men might see his hand burned before his body was touched. His body did so abide the burning of the flame, with such constancy and steadfastness, that standing always in one place, without moving his body, he seemed to move no more than the stake to which he was bound: his eyes were lifted up unto heaven, and often times he repeated his "unworthy right hand," so long as his voice would suffer him: and using often the words of Stephen, Lord Jesus receive my spirit; in the greatness of the flame he gave up the ghost.

It was an eye-witness, an upholder of the old faith, who testified to Cranmer's unflinching courage in the fire, and his stretching his hand to the flames with the words "this hand hath offended." The surrenders and recantations of the immediate past were thus redeemed by a brave end and a testimony to his sincere convictions.

On the very day that Cranmer died, Reginald Pole celebrated his first mass in the Grey Friars Church at Greenwich, where he had been ordained priest the day before, and on the morrow

CRANMER'S TRIAL AND EXECUTION

in the same church he was consecrated Archbishop of Canterbury. He had just completed his fifty-sixth year and was in poor health, and the task of re-establishing the papal authority in England was beyond his strength or Mary's. He was soon even deprived of the Pope's support. Paul IV (Caraffa) was soon at war with Philip, who returned to England for his second and last visit in March, 1557, wishing to implicate England in the war, and a month later Paul cancelled Pole's office as legate, appointing Friar Peto in his place and making him a cardinal. Pole was even cited to Rome, and detected that there was an insinuation of his being a heretic. Mary's unhappiness increased, and there were reasons in plenty for it—her husband's absence and neglect of her and his quarrel with the Papacy, her childlessness in spite of her sanguine and repeated hopes that she was with child, the loss of Calais in the war into which England had been drawn in the interests of Spain, and, above all, the ominous signs of growing resistance to her ecclesiastical policy. The leaders of the reform movement had, indeed, been put to death, save those who had fled abroad, but the burning of obscure lay-folk, including women, which continued to the end of the reign, rather confirmed the faith of the adherents of the movement than terrorized them. London, in those days more important relatively to the country at large than it has since become, proved ungovernable, and in other towns and throughout Eastern England the sympathisers with reform increased. There had been little in the early treatment of Mary and her Spanish mother to give her that robust patriotism which came naturally to her half-sister. For lack of wise English advisers she had leant much on the advice of the Emperor Charles V in his lifetime and on that of her cousin Reginald Pole, but neither of them realized at a distance the changed climate of English opinion. Mary's English supporters belonged to the old rather than to the new aristocracy; their day was passing, while the power of the trading classes and the towns was growing. Some of Mary's statesmen not only belonged to the old order but were themselves aged or ailing. The younger men, such as William Cecil, might accommodate themselves for the moment, but would find their more congenial employment in the service of Elizabeth and the new order. And so Mary died in the early morning of 17th November, 1558, and some twelve hours later Archbishop Pole died in his sleep. Both had been conscientious and single-minded in their devotion to the Roman Church, but the cause was already failing before the head of the State and the head of the Church in England died in the course of a single day.

Chapter Eleven

Epilogue

THE next reign determined how far the Reformation would take permanent root among the English people and how much of Cranmer's spirit would continue to inform it. The character of the Tudor monarchy gave almost unlimited power of direction to the sovereign, and Elizabeth had as forceful a personality as Henry VIII and elicited from the English people a more devoted and whole-hearted loyalty than he. Edward VI was but a boy in the hands of powerful ministers; Mary was but half English, and her Spanish marriage as well as the ruthless persecutions lost her the popularity which had greeted her at her accession; but Elizabeth was "pure English," and she knew well how to exploit to the full the flowing tide of national feeling. Like her father, and unlike her sister Mary, her interests and driving motives were political more than religious. She believed, as most political thinkers of her day did, that the unity of the nation would be strengthened by as large a degree as possible of religious unity, and that it would be disastrously weakened by religious faction, which might even invite foreign intervention and overthrow the dynasty.

Elizabeth, in the twenty-five years of her troubled life had already learnt the need of restraint and circumspection. She was surrounded by persons who had so compromised themselves by conformity to the successive changes in religion that their sincerity was not to be counted on. She needed also to keep a very watchful eye on the European situation. She did not at once reveal her ecclesiastical policy but kept the Emperor and the King of France and their ambassadors all guessing. Even the new Pope, Pius V, did not despair of her and addressed her in a letter of greeting as his "dear daughter." Philip sought her hand and, since peace was not yet concluded with France, she needed his alliance. The English people, too, were left in doubt for some months. The Marian bishops continued in office and officiated at Mary's obsequies and Elizabeth's coronation and in the royal chapel. A Proclamation, issued within six weeks of the new queen's accession, ordered that "until consultation may be had by Parliament," such services and ceremonies should continue in use as were "already used and by law received," save only that the epistle and gospel for the day, the creed, the Lord's Prayer and the Ten Commandments might be used in English, and "the common Litany used at this present in her majesty's own chapel" (with the offensive allusion to the Pope now for good and all omitted). Elizabeth could use the Royal Supremacy to deal with the immediate present by proclamations and injunctions but, like her father, she was determined to place the onus of religious change on Council and Parliament. Convocation was already so much robbed of its ancient authority that she could afford to override or ignore it, but in an episcopal church she would need bishops to bear the burden of executing any changes that were determined.

From the moment of her accession, Elizabeth had taken Sir William Cecil to be her principal Secretary of State, and a few weeks later she had appointed Cecil's brother-in-law, Sir Nicholas Bacon, to be Lord Keeper of the Great Seal. The Council was still a rather uncertain mixture of adherents of the old faith and the new, but by a few judicious changes and by the readiness of many members to go with the tide, she might soon reckon on its support. Her first Parliament, which met on 25th January, 1559, had, before it rose in April, after much discussion passed two acts of supreme importance. The Act of Supremacy repealed the heresy acts and restored the Royal Supremacy, giving to the Crown full visitatorial rights over the church and imposing an oath of supremacy to be taken by all officeholders in Church and State. The oath, without naming the Pope, required the utter renunciation of "all foreign jurisdictions"; the Queen was designated "the only supreme Governor of this realm, as well in all spiritual or ecclesiastical things or causes, as temporal." The title "Supreme Head," last borne unwillingly by Mary in the first year of her reign, was exchanged for the less offensive "Supreme Governor," which Elizabeth was careful to explain soon after as claiming no "power of ministry of divine offices in the Church." As the thirty-seventh Article states:

> We give not to our princes the ministering either of God's word or of sacraments, the which thing the Injunctions also lately set forth by Elizabeth our Queen doth most plainly testify.

The Act of Uniformity enjoined the use from the following Midsummer Day of the Prayer Book of 1552, with a few significant changes. The offensive reference to the Bishop of Rome was expunged from the Litany. The Black Rubric of 1552, which had been inserted by the Council without having been submitted to Parliament, was properly omitted, and when it was re-introduced in 1662, its language was altered in a less Zwinglian direction. In the administration to communicants the words from the first Prayer Book, which were inherited from the Sarum rite, were now combined

EPILOGUE

with those of the second; the undoubted purpose of this change was to conciliate the Catholic-minded, while not antagonizing those who held a more Protestant view.

The Marian bishops spoke in the House of Lords against both these Acts while they were at discussion, and voted against them, so that it was only by the votes of the temporal peers that the measures were carried in that house. At the same time Convocation, over which Bonner presided, as there was as yet no Archbishop of Canterbury, professed its faith in the traditional doctrine of the Eucharist and in papal supremacy. There was no escape from a wholesale re-manning of the episcopate, if the changes ordered by these Acts were to take effect. There had been a remarkable mortality among the bishops in the last year of Mary's reign and within a few weeks of her death, so that ten sees were vacant, including the archbishopric of Canterbury. Elizabeth summoned the surviving bishops in June, and they were given three weeks to decide whether they would take the Oath of Supremacy. All but two refused. They were then in June and July deprived of their sees, Tunstall's case being postponed till 28th September, in the hope that so moderate a man might be won over. Bonner was sent to the Marshalsea, where he died nine years later. Most of the others, after a short time in the Tower, were committed to the charge of an Anglican bishop. Tunstall, for whom Elizabeth, like most people, had a real regard, was spared any imprisonment and was sent to Lambeth Palace, where the archbishop-elect was already in residence; he was there treated as a guest rather than as a prisoner and received honourable burial when he died at the age of eighty-five after being there only nine weeks. Heath, late Archbishop of York, was allowed to live on his own estate at Chobham, in Surrey, and was there visited by the Queen more than once in the twenty years that still remained to him. David Poole also was allowed to live in one of his own farms, and four others died at liberty. Watson, formerly Bishop of Lincoln, was released after some years of captivity but, it being discovered that he was corresponding with Douai, he was committed to the stricter confinement of Wisbech Castle, where he died in 1580. Two escaped abroad; Pates went to Louvain, and Goldwell, who settled at Rome, took an active interest in the missions to England, and died at Rome in 1585, the last survivor of the Marian bishops. The treatment of the bishops in Mary's reign and Elizabeth's may be compared. Under Mary, fourteen were deprived, including five who had been intruded into sees whose previous occupants were still living; under Elizabeth, fifteen were deprived. Under Elizabeth few of the

EPILOGUE

deprived bishops suffered long imprisonment, and none were executed; under Mary, five were burnt.

Elizabeth was in no hurry to fill the vacancies. In the second half of 1559, two bishops deprived under Mary, Barlow and Scory, were appointed to Chichester and Hereford; Bishop Coverdale was unwilling to have a bishopric again. It was of the greatest importance to find the right man for Canterbury, and Elizabeth made an admirable choice. Matthew Parker, a scholar like Cranmer, was as unwilling as he to assume the primacy in such difficult times; he pleaded ill-health, love of study and a retired life, but he reluctantly undertook the burden. He was elected by the chapter of Canterbury on 1st August, 1559, in accordance with the *conge d'elire* and the letter missive directing his appointment, but there was much delay over his consecration, Tunstall and others refusing to officiate. In the end it was not till thirteen months after Elizabeth's accession that he was consecrated in Lambeth Palace Chapel by Barlow and Hodgkin, who had been consecrated with the Sarum rite twenty-two years before, and by Scory and Coverdale, who had been consecrated in 1551 with the Edwardian ordinal; three of the four consecrated bishops had returned from exile. In the next three months eleven bishops were consecrated by Parker with other bishops assisting.

There was very much less difficulty in securing the continuity of service of the parochial clergy than of the bishops. Nearly all of them retained their benefices; out of over 9,000 less than 200 were displaced for refusing to take the Oath of Supremacy, and perhaps about as many more were deprived (not always for doctrinal reasons) or resigned in the next six years. Many of the older of them had begun their clerical life as monks or friars and were not well fitted for parochial duties. There was for long a scarcity of able preachers, and, to fill the parochial vacancies, too many men of slender capacities were too hastily ordained.

At least four of the new bishops had taken refuge in Germany or Switzerland during the Marian persecution, and one of Parker's greatest difficulties was to co-operate with bishops and deans who had come under strong Calvinist influence during their time abroad. The efficiency of the Genevan Church and the personal ascendancy of John Calvin had impressed many of the English exiles, although some of them had made only minor concessions to the criticism of their Calvinist neighbours. The acute differences between the English exiles, which would later be painfully reflected in the Elizabethan Church, are best illustrated in *A Brief Discourse of the Troubles at Frankfort*, 1554–1558. The magistracy of Frankfort-on-the-Main granted White Ladies Church in that city for the alternate use of French and English religious exiles. The first Englishmen arriving there in the summer of 1554, were predominantly Calvinist, and they organized themselves into a church, with a service on the Calvinistic model. They sent letters to the Englishmen settled at Zurich, Strasburg, Emden, and other towns to come to Frankfort as a rallying-point of English Protestantism, and they appointed as joint ministers John Knox of Geneva, to meet the wishes of the Calvinists, and Thomas Lever of Zurich to satisfy the Anglicans. For a while there was a compromise, but the Anglican element was growing stronger and Knox appealed to Calvin for his opinion on the Book of Common Prayer. Calvin, who had seen only Knox's scoffing account of it, found in it many questionable things, but thought them "for a season to be tolerated," though he wondered that any should still "so greatly delight in the leavings of Popish dregs," except that "they love the things whereunto they are accustomed." But he counselled Knox not to be "fierce" over those whose "infirmity will not suffer them to ascend a higher step."

The truce was broken when a fresh wave of exiles arrived in March, 1554, soon after the burnings had begun in England, and made an

Anglican majority at Frankfort. Their leader, Richard Cox, afterwards to be a bishop, was soon at issue with Knox, and he was supported by three doctors and thirteen bachelors of divinity. The Prayer Book men wanted the Frankfort congregation to "have the face of an English church," and the struggle between Cox and Knox ended in Knox returning to Geneva, and many of his supporters migrating there or to Basel. Even at Frankfort the Anglicans were in part persuaded by the German Protestants and in part yielded for the sake of peace, but, as they informed Calvin, they made many concessions, surrendering confirmation, kneeling at communion, and the use of the surplice, but adhering to the Communion Office. It may well be imagined that the return of the exiles to England would make grave difficulties for Parker when he sought to ensure uniformity; the Marian bishop who preached at Mary's burial had foretold what notions would be brought in by "the wolves coming out of Geneva." A motion introduced on 13th February, 1563, in the Lower House of Convocation to make kneeling at communion optional, to abolish crossing the child at baptism, to abrogate all saints' days, and to remove organs, was defeated by only one vote. The archbishop could only with great difficulty secure obedience to the minimum requirements of the law, and he

EPILOGUE

could not count on the loyal support of all the diocesan bishops. He did, however, all that he could, short of ruthless disciplinary measures, to ensure that the Church of England should preserve the reverent administration of the sacraments, the decent vesting of the holy table, and the strict observance of the Prayer Book.

The Elizabethan Prayer Book ordered the use of such vestments as had been in use in the second year of Edward's reign, but the archbishop realized that, in the face of much opposition, he must be content with a minimum requirement of the cope for the three ministers at the altar in cathedral churches, and "a comely surplice with sleeves" in the parish church. The Injunctions of 1559 also provided for the maintenance of "the laudable science of music" in the choral foundations of the cathedral churches, and for the use of plainsong, and at the beginning or end of common prayers "there may be sung an hymn, in the best sort of melody and music that may be conveniently devised." The Prayer Book rubrics also provided for the singing of some parts of the liturgical services such as the *Gloria in Excelsis*. A faithful fulfilment of the Prayer Book differentiated the Anglican service from the Calvinistic model and made evident the intention to retain much of the traditional order. It was not to be expected that insistence on the prescribed use of liturgy would satisfy the extremists. It was already obvious that many Puritans would continue to hope that the Reformation would be carried further and the Church be remodelled on Calvinist lines, but Archbishop Parker, like Cranmer, had a respect for tradition and would not give way. It should be noted that the Puritan element was also strongly represented in the Council, and still more so in Parliament, but when Strickland in 1571 introduced a motion for alterations in religion he was ordered by the Council not to appear again in his place. On similar occasions later the Queen showed her displeasure; she was not minded to depute the exercise of ecclesiastical discipline to Parliament.

While the Anglican system was threatened by Puritan attempts to destroy the delicate balance between old and new, there was also a very large part of the population, perhaps even a majority, which clung in their hearts to the old faith. They had seen with dismay the wholesale and often lawless iconoclasm, the destruction of familiar and well-loved objects of devotion, and the introduction of a service-book which seemed to them bare, deficient, and perhaps heretical. By avoiding the extremes of continental Protestantism, and preserving much of the old ways of worship, it was hoped that many would gradually accept the new order. The English spirit of compromise

EPILOGUE

was in favour of such accommodation, and in fact the Anglican Church won the allegiance of very many who had conformed in Mary's reign. Others, to avoid the fines for not attending the parish church, practised occasional conformity. This practice, however, became impossible for those of sincere devotion to Rome when on 25th February, 1570, Pius V issued his Bull, *Regnans in excelsis*; in the small hours of 15th May, one John Felton, husband of a former maid of honour to Queen Mary, affixed a copy of the Bull on the gates of the Bishop of London's palace and paid for it with his life. The Bull not only excommunicated Elizabeth, as it well might do, seeing that she had "forbidden the prelates, clergy and people to acknowledge the Church of Rome" and "the observance of the true religion," but it also absolved the people from allegiance to her.

> "Moreover, we declare that she has forfeited her pretended title to the aforesaid kingdom, to all and every right, dignity and privilege; we also declare that the nobles, the subjects, and the people, who have taken any oath to her are for ever released from that oath, and from every obligation of allegiance, fealty, and obedience, as we now by these letters release them, and deprive the said Elizabeth of her pretended right to the throne, and every other right whatsoever aforesaid; we command all

and singular the nobles, the people subject to her, and others aforesaid, never to venture to obey her monitions, mandates, and laws."

The speedy collapse of a rising towards the end of 1569 in favour of the old religion and of Mary Queen of Scots, in the north, the most feudal and most conservative part of England, seemed to show that there was not very general support for armed resistance to Elizabeth's government. Mary had taken refuge in England in May of the previous year, and was virtually a prisoner in Tutbury Castle, Shropshire. On the suppression of the rebellion many of the participants were hanged.

Philip II and other Catholic sovereigns questioned the wisdom of the Bull, and it was a cause of painful embarrassment to Roman Catholics in England. For the most part they had been and continued to be as loyal subjects as any to Queen Elizabeth, but for the rest of the reign their loyalty was liable to question and the penalties, now increased, for practising their religion were more rigorously executed. There was no persecution in Elizabeth's reign till her later years when the Queen believed there was imminent political danger. New laws in 1571 made it treasonable to deny Elizabeth's title to the throne or to call her a heretic, or to receive any Bull or objects blessed by the Pope. The continued presence of

EPILOGUE

the Scottish queen in England increased the fear of plots connected with her. When from about 1580 priests who had been trained in Rome or in the English College at Douai, began to come into England to sustain the faith of their adherents, they were ruthlessly run to ground by pursuivants and arrested. One of the first to arrive was Cuthbert Mayne; dressed in lay clothes, he passed as steward to a recusant Cornish squire and ministered to other recusants in that neighbourhood till he was arrested. An obsolete Papal Bull was found among his belongings, and this was technically high treason, although the Act was hardly intended to treat so venial an offence with the penalty of death. As the judges disagreed, the matter was referred to the Council, which ordered his execution. He had admitted in answer to a question that he thought it the duty of all Catholics to assist an invader; this is the sole, if sufficient, justification for his execution, though not for the barbarity with which it was carried out.

This first execution was followed a few years later by that of the Douai priests, Robert Parsons and Edward Campion, Jesuits, who arrived in 1580. Parsons, after spending some sixteen months in England and running the gravest risks, escaped to Normandy, and was later to be active in promoting the Spanish invasion of England.

His companion, Edward Campion, a man of lovable character and wholly free from political designs, was betrayed after a year's stay in England, brought to the Tower, three times put to the rack, and then, with seven others, tried for raising a sedition to dethrone the Queen. The trial was as unfair, says Hallam, "as any, perhaps, that can be found in our books." After their conviction, when the judge asked if they had anything to say against the sentence of death, Campion made this notable reply:

> "The only thing that we have now to say is that if our religion do make us traitors we are worthy to be condemned; but otherwise are and have been true subjects as ever the Queen had. In condemning us you condemn all your own ancestors—all the ancient priests, bishops and kings—all that was once the glory of England, the island of saints and the most devoted child of the see of Peter. For what have we taught, however you may qualify it with the odious name of treason, that they did not uniformly teach? To be condemned with these old lights—not of England only, but of the world—by their degenerate descendants is both gladness and glory to us. God lives; posterity will live; their judgment is not so liable to corruption as that of those who are now going to sentence us to death."

Campion and his companions were hanged, drawn and quartered on 1st December, 1581.

EPILOGUE

Several Acts with severe penalties for harbouring Jesuits and seminary priests and for hearing Mass were passed in the years from 1571 to 1587. None-the-less, the seminary missioners continued to come to England with heroic devotion to their faith. Some 280 in all suffered the penalty of death in the later years of Elizabeth's reign.

It was the policy of the Queen's ministers to represent that these men suffered, not for their religion, but for treason. But, for all that Francis Bacon might say in defence of the penal laws, it was never easy, and it was not always attempted by the Government, to distinguish between those who were "Papists in conscience" and those who were "Papists in treasonable faction." It is indubitable that many of the victims were, like Campion, wholly guiltless of treasonable intention, and suffered the death penalty for preaching a religion that was proscribed. There were, however, conspiracies which the government was obliged to deal with severely; some of them were designs for replacing Elizabeth by Mary Stuart on the English throne with the help of foreign armies. Mary's complicity in Babington's conspiracy brought her to the block on 8th February, 1587. The repercussions to this event were immediate. Pope Sixtus V renewed his predecessor's sentence of deposition of the bastard

Elizabeth, who had added to her other crimes by the murdering of "numbers of holy priests and other Catholic persons" and the "late cruelty used against the most gracious Princess, Mary Queen of Scotland"; and he called upon the faithful in England to support the approaching invasion of the country by the Duke of Parma. But while some of the exiles fostered it, the Roman Catholics in England were as loyal as any when the Armada was sighted off the English coast on 19th July, 1588. Its defeat put an end to any likelihood of a restoration of Roman obedience in England by force.

Meanwhile the relations of the Church of England with the more thorough-going Puritans had not improved. Few, indeed, contemplated or effected separation; their more general hope was to transform the Church to the Genevan type. In particular there was a movement among beneficed clergymen to superimpose on the Church a Presbyterian doctrine and discipline. The Queen reprimanded Parker's successor, Archbishop Grindal, for not suppressing the "Prophesyings" and the meetings for devotional reading, and for introducing the discipline in the eastern counties. There was much earnestness and piety in the movement, and it had an able advocate of the Presbyterian system in Thomas Cartwright, a Cambridge professor. In 1588 began

EPILOGUE

the series of spirited and audacious Marprelate tracts, privately printed and widely circulated. Various Puritans whose writings were regarded as seditious under the Statute of 1581, were brought before the courts. Greenwood and Barrow, who had joined the separatist movement begun by Robert Browne, were hanged at Tyburn on 6th April, 1593, and seven weeks later, John Penry, regarded since as the founder of Welsh dissent, suffered the same cruel fate. Many who thought as they did found it safer to go to the Low Countries. Several generations would pass before the practice of religious toleration was generally adopted. It has been well said by the present Bishop of Durham that "the Elizabethan Settlement is an accepted and justifiable description, but there was much that it did not settle."

It was the one cardinal error in Richard Hooker's great work, *Of the Laws of Ecclesiastical Polity*, published towards the close of Elizabeth's reign, that he hoped the national church to be practically co-extensive with the nation. It would become increasingly evident that the Church would comprise the majority of the people, but that strongly held convictions would hold back important minorities, both of those who rejected the English Reformation and of those who thought it had not gone far enough. In other respects, Hooker's book was far the ablest vindication of the Anglican *via media* that had yet appeared, a "reasoned positive defence of Anglican order and liturgy." In language of grave dignity, and with a charity and restraint that have never been equalled in theological controversy, Hooker upheld the middle way as nearer to truth than either extreme. The Puritans looked to Scripture for the sole ground of every detail of church order and government. Hooker allowed as fully as they the sufficiency of Scripture for what was necessary to salvation, but maintained that for the ordering of church life it gave no complete guidance, and that respect should be had to tradition, "the mind and purpose of the old Fathers," and to "sound reason." Hooker's argument had been anticipated by Cranmer who, in protesting against the view that what is not commanded in Scripture is against Scripture, said: "This saying is a subversion of all order as well in religion as in common policy." That a belief or a ceremony was inherited from the medieval church was with Hooker no objection to its adoption, if it could be shown to be inherently reasonable and not conflicting with any principle enunciated in the New Testament. It was the strongest possible line of defence and of positive statement for his own day, and, though it is necessarily less convincing in our day when some of his postulates have come to be widely denied, it did more to give the Anglican church an intellectual justification than anything hitherto printed. Hooker's thought supplied the groundwork for the great Caroline divines of the next generation. The Church of England claimed to rest its defence on the fundamental principles of Catholic Christianity and on sound learning as well as on the supreme authority of the Bible. By the next generation churchmen were surer of their ground than was possible in the turmoil of the Reformation age; the piety of a Lancelot Andrewes or a George Herbert was securely anchored in the worship and ordered life of the Church, while there had gradually grown up a loyalty of the laity which would survive the storms and catastrophic defeats of the Civil War and the Commonwealth.

It may be considered, in conclusion, what is the relation of Cranmer to the later history of the English Church? He had done more than any man to secure free and unfettered access to the English Bible, which was to be the foundation of the average Englishman's religion and a criterion of what was taught and practised in his church. He had fathered a Book of Common Prayer which, while abandoning some ceremonies that had come to be regarded as superfluous or leading to popular superstition, and introducing some features from new contemporary forms of service, had in the main preserved the accustomed church order and many of the "ancient" prayers consecrated by the Christian experience of many centuries. He had stood for decency and order in public worship, and had laboured with uncommon skill to express it in language of dignity and beauty. John Keble valued the Prayer Book especially for giving to the Church "a sober standard of feeling" in matters of practical religion. And if in the Prayer Book of 1552, more was sacrificed of ancient and approved liturgical use than need have been, each revision—in the reigns of Elizabeth, James I and Charles II—has recovered things that have improved the service-book. The Forty-two Articles of Religion of 1553, for which Cranmer must bear the chief responsibility, were reshaped, with some omissions and additions, in 1571, as the Thirty-nine Articles. Sixteenth century confessions of faith necessarily bear the marks of that age, and many of the controversies have ceased to interest later generations. But the Thirty-nine Articles compare favourably with the continental confessions. They are less minutely articulated and avoid the extremes of the Calvinist statements; they were intended to win the assent of as many as possible and therefore allow of greater latitude in interpretation than such doctrinal statements commonly do. John Henry Newman, in his Anglican days was by no means the first to discover the mediating and temperate

EPILOGUE

character of the English Articles; that was already being urged exactly four centuries before the beginning of the Oxford Movement. In any case the religious life of the English people has been far more influenced by their familiarity with the Prayer Book than by the Articles. It is also to be remembered that the English Reformation has never labelled those who accepted it as Cranmerians, like the Lutherans and Calvinists. Cranmer gave it the best direction he could, but his personal opinions have not enslaved those that came after him. His spirit and charitable temper have served the generations, but his letter has not bound them. There are words of his which have found a place in every edition of the Prayer Book from 1549 to our own day: "Christ's Gospel . . . is a religion to God, not in bondage of the figure or shadow, but in the freedom of spirit."

List of Books

The following books will be found useful for further reading :—

The Works of Cranmer, Parker Society

James Gairdner : *The English Church from the Accession of Henry VIII to the Death of Mary*

W. H. Frere : *The English Church in the Reigns of Elizabeth and James I*

H. A. L. Fisher : *History of England, 1485-1547*

A. F. Pollard : *History of England, 1547-1603*

A. F. Pollard : *Thomas Cranmer*

A. F. Pollard : *Henry VIII*

A. F. Pollard : *Wolsey*

A. F. Pollard : *England under Protector Somerset*

J. E. Neale : *Queen Elizabeth*

J. A. Froude : *History of England*

Geoffrey Baskerville : *The English Monks and the Dissolution of the Monasteries*

A. L. Rowse : *Tudor Cornwall*

A. F. Scott Pearson : *Thomas Cartwright and Elizabethan Puritanism*

M. M. Knapper : *Tudor Puritanism*

W. Schenk : *Reginald Pole*

Proctor and Frere : *The English Prayer Book*

Index

A

Act dissolving Chantries, 1547, 102
— forbidding payment to Rome of Peter's Pence, 1534, 54, 56, 62, 64
— for dissolution of lesser monasteries, 1536, 65 *ff.*
— for dissolution of greater monasteries, 1539, 68
— in absolute restraint of Annates, 1534, 54, 62
— in conditional restraint of Annates, 1532, 29, 34, 51
— in restraint of appeals, 1533, 30, 52, 62
— of Submission of Clergy, 1534, 54, 61
— of Succession, First and Second, 1534, 55, 62, 135
— of Supremacy, 1534, 59, 64
— of Supremacy, 1559, 163
— of Uniformity, 1549, 105, 110
— — 1552, 105, 141
— — 1559, 164
Anabaptists, 77
Anne of Cleves, 85
Arthur, Prince of Wales, 21, 26, 28
Articles, Forty-two, 128-129, 182
— Six, 82-4, 86, 100, 111, 127, 137
— Thirty-nine, 182
— Ten, 78, 81
Augsburg, Confession of, 83

B

Bernard, St., 9
Bible, Cranmer's, 91
— Great, 18, 80, 91
— Matthew's, 90, 91, 147
Bishops' Book (*see Institution of Christian Man*)
Black Rubric, 130, 164
Boleyn, Anne, 21, 23, 24, 27, 33, 37, 38, 55, 62, 97
Book of Common Prayer, 94, 103 *ff.*, 110, 118 *ff.*, 139, 141, 164-165, 169 *ff.*, 181-183

C

Cambridge, University of, part in Reformation, 13-15
Campeggio, Cardinal, 25, 26
Cartwright, Thomas, 178

INDEX

Catherine of Aragon, 1, 21-24, 26, 29, 30, 37-38, 42, 53-55, 97, 142
Cecil, William, 136, 140, 160, 163
Clement VII (Pope), 3, 23-26, 29, 33-34, 37
Colet, John, 4, 8, 9
Convocation, recognition by of Henry VIII as Supreme Head of Church, 46
Coverdale, Miles, 13, 90, 93, 107, 167
CRANMER, Thomas, and Book of Common Prayer, 103 ff., 122 ff.
— and Continental Reformers, 84, 118 ff.
— and Dissolution of Monasteries, 70-71
— and Doctrine of Eucharist, 83, 124 ff., 144-145
— and future of Church of England, 181-183
— and Great Bible, 89 ff.
— and Litany, 93 ff.
— and *Order of Communion*, 101-102
— and succession to Edward VI, 134-138
— attainder, 140
— birth, 14
— committed to Tower, 140
— declares Henry VIII's marriage to Catherine null and void, 37
— examination of, by Commissioners, 143 ff.
— examination of, by Privy Council, 87
— execution of, 155 ff.
— first marriage, 14
— made Archbishop, 34
— opposition to Six Articles, 82
— plea for Cromwell's life, 85
— recantation by, 154
— responsibility for Acts of Reformation Parliament, 61-63
— second marriage, 31
— trial of, 149 ff.
— with Emperor, 30 ff.
Cromwell, Thomas, 6, 20, 43, 47, 56-57, 60, 64-65, 66-67, 69, 70. 78, 85-86, 88, 116

D

Dudley, John (Earl of Warwick, Duke of Northumberland), 99, 112, 114-118, 132-135, 138

E

Edward VI, 93, 96, 98, 99, 102, 103, 113, 133-134, 136-137, 161
Elizabeth (Tudor), 37, 97, 133, 138, 160-163, 165-167, 172-174, 177
Erasmus, Desiderius, 4, 5, 10, 15, 20

INDEX

F

Fisher, John, 10-12, 44, 53, 56-59, 72, 155
Frith, John, 76-77

G

Gardiner, Stephen, 20, 26-27, 36, 47, 49, 50, 74, 77, 83, 85, 97, 100, 106, 109, 114, 115, 116, 125, 127, 128, 129, 141, 145, 146, 147
Grey, Lady Jane, 133-134, 137-138, 140, 142

H

Henry VIII, *passim*
Hertford, Earl of (*see* Seymour, Edward)
Holbein, 59
Hooker, Richard, 179, 180, 181
Hunne, Richard, 7, 8

I

Indulgences, 10
Institution of a Christian Man, 81

K

Kett's rebellion, 112
Knox, John, 130, 133, 169, 170

L

Lambert, John, 84
Latimer, Hugh, 13, 69, 71, 80-82, 90, 103, 140, 143, 148
Leach, A. F., 102
Leo X (Pope), 12
Litany, Cranmer's, 94
Lollards, 8-9, 11
Luther, Martin, 3, 5, 8, 10, 12, 17, 76

M

Mary, Queen of Scots, 174-175, 177-178
Mary (Tudor), 22, 23, 26, 37, 56, 67, 74, 75, 96, 114, 116, 132, 134, 136, 138-139, 142, 146, 149, 152, 159, 160-161, 166-167
Melancthon, 85, 119
Monasteries, 68
More, Thomas, 5, 8, 10, 16, 40, 42-43, 51, 56, 57-59, 72, 88, 107

INDEX

N

Norfolk, Duke of, 82, 98
Northumberland, Duke of (*see* Dudley, John)

O

Oxford, University of, 14, 28, 33

P

Papacy, 2
Parker, Matthew, 112, 167-168, 170, 172
Parliament, composition of, 41
Petition of Commons, 1532, 47 *ff.*
Philip II (of Spain), 142, 146, 174
Pilgrimage of Grace, 67
Pole, Reginald, 3, 111, 119, 141-142, 146, 148, 158-160
Pollard, A. F., 109

R

Regnans in excelsis (Papal Bull), 173
Renaissance, 4
Reynolds, Dr. R., 60-61
Ridley, Nicholas, 125, 140, 143, 148

S

Seymour, Edward (Earl of Hertford and Duke of Somerset), 97, 98 *ff.*, 112, 114, 115, 116, 120, 121
Seymour, Jane, 97
Somerset, Duke of (*see* Seymour, Edward)

T

Treasons Act, 1534, 57, 58, 60, 63, 100
Tyndale, William, 15, 16, 17, 89, 90

U

Utopia, 42

W

Warwick, Earl of (*see* Dudley, John)
Wolsey, Thomas, 6, 7, 12, 13, 20, 23, 24, 25, 26, 31, 39, 40, 46, 65, 69, 88